# THE Unexplained

# Creatures from Elsewhere

## Weird animals that no-one can explain

## Editor: Peter Brookesmith

CHARTWELL
BOOKS, INC.

**Acknowledgements**
Photographs were supplied by Acorn Photographics, Aldus
Books, Associated Press, *c.* Artia/Zdenek Burian, Herbert
Ballard, John Beckett, Bettman Archive, Janet and Colin
Bord, Bord Failte, BBC Hulton Picture Library, Cambridge
University Collection of Aerial Photography, Jean-Loup
Charmet, John Cleare, Bruce Coleman, Peter Costello, Tim
Dinsdale Colin Edwards, Robert Estall, Mary Evans Picture
Library, Joel Finler Collection, Ed Fletcher, Werner
Forman, Fortean Picture Library, Paul H. Fugleberg,
Arlene B. Gaal, Robert Harding, B. Heuvelmans, Hans
Hinz, Michael Holford, Mrs F. Holliday, Image Bank, L.
Allen Klope, Laing Art Gallery, Frank W. Lane, London
Express, Mansell Collection, Natural Science Photos, Peter
Newark, Popperfoto, Press Association, Royal Academy,
Royal Geographical Society, Royal Irish Academy, Ronald
Sheridan Photo Library, Adrian Shine, Paul Snelgrove,
Frank Spooner, Mai Sullivan, Syndication International,
Tate Gallery, Theosophical Society, John Topham Picture
Library, Udreasfeavifen, UPI, Washington Post, Zenka
Woodward Picture Library.

**Consultants:**
Professor A J Ellinson
Dr J Allen Hynek
Brian Inglis
Colin Wilson

# Contents

# Introduction

THERE ARE TWO ANIMALS that are not to be found in any zoo but that must be known to almost everyone in the Western world: the Loch Ness monster and the bigfoot (or yeti, as it's known in the Himalayas). But how many people have heard of the flying black batwoman of Vietnam, the *peiste* of the Irish loughs, or know the full story of the Minnesota Iceman? You will learn of all these things in this book – and consider too whether that creature of legend, the werewolf, may not still be alive and well in Europe today.

But we are presenting here something more besides: that is not merely a collection of spine chilling tales and outlandish stories – though many reports of 'unknown' animals are far from reassuring and often very bizarre indeed. What these chapters offer are careful examinations of the reports and photographs of the creatures, informed speculations about their nature and origins, and, where appropriate, a discussion of the *kind* of reality such weird entities may inhabit. For in dealing with some of the more extraordinary of these reports, made by reliable witnesses with no apparent desire for notoriety or profit, there often appears to be no alternative explanation for the events described than some kind of parallel reality, some other dimension, from which these creatures inexplicably and elusively emerge, if ever so briefly, into the light of our world.

## Legends of the Loch

That possibility does seem rather remote, however, when we are dealing with our two most famous examples. Certainly, it's true that the first reports from Scotland of something very strange swimming about in Loch Ness first filtered out only in the 1930s, following the cutting of a new road alongside the long, gloomy stretch of water. But for a hundred years or more before that, the local people had known that *something* was there. (And they were in no doubt either that there was something very peculiar lurking in the waters of 1000-feet-deep Loch Morar, 40 miles or so away to the west. But the shy denizens of that water have never had the flocks of passing strangers, publicity seekers, charlatans or even plain scientists to draw attention to them in the way that the tenants of Loch Ness have.) And, as ever, the likelihood of getting to the bottom of the mystery in Loch Ness was long kept at bay by an irritating trickle of spurious photographs of such things as posts with socks hanging off them, as well as honestly mistaken photographs of standing waves, wakes of long-passed boats, or drifting logs. Few serious investigators would go near the place, leaving it prey to cranks and the merely curious.

It wasn't simply the odour of bad publicity that kept away the biologists and ecologists who should have been there all the time, however. There were practical reasons too: Loch Ness is a vast stretch of water, and it is impossible to see very far into it because of the peat that stains it. Not until the development of sophisticated forms of sonar during the 1960s was it possible to employ a really effective method of detection in the loch. One of the more imaginative notions for tracking Nessie involved using trained dolphins to home in on a sonar contact and have them photograph it!

But even if the means had been available earlier, would the scientific establishment have taken up the challenge? Probably not, if only because in this century scientists have displayed a depressing tendency to imagine that, having mapped the globe and spread himself into all its corners, modern man has discovered all its wonders. (With a similar extravagance of closed mind, the then director of the US Patent Office in 1899 urged President McKinley to close it forthwith, on the principle that 'Everything that can be invented has been invented.') It seemed ridiculous that an undiscovered and unnamed animal could have been sitting in the civilised world's back yard and have gone unnoticed so long. Embarrassed, and nervous of the more eccentric devotees of the loch's mysterious inhabitants, scientists became as shy as any monster of the deep.

But when they do venture near the loch, even the most respected of scientists can come away with egg on his face. The famous naturalist Sir Peter Scott may have been a little over-enthusiastic in his interpretation of 'monster' photographs taken in Loch Ness, but that did not prevent him forging ahead to give the ostensible animal a scientific name – *Nessiteras rhombopteryx*. Spend a little time rearranging the letters of this honest attempt to label Nessie and you will find they also spell the words 'monster hoax by Sir Peter S'.

Nonetheless, serious and disciplined research into whatever dwells in Loch Ness is well under way in the 1980s. Not as much, unfortunately, can be said for the world's other star monster, the bigfoot, sasquatch or yeti.

## Abominable mystery

Once again the evidence from local folklore is extremely strong and remarkably consistent, whether it comes from the Himalayas, the Canadian Rockies or deep in the United States. There really does seem to be some kind of man-like beast shambling around in the shadows of civilisation. Or perhaps there are several kinds: for reports come in from all over the globe, from the wastes of Siberia and the chill peaks of Nepal to the suburbs of America. It seems reasonable to suppose that there may be regional variations of the hairy man-beast. So much, however, must remain speculation, for not one of the creatures has been captured or shot. (Remembering the fate of some rare species whose last surviving examples were shot simply to be stuffed and displayed in museums, perhaps we should be grateful that none have yet been hunted down, for all the loss to human knowledge.)

That simple fact must lead the honest observer to wonder

if something else has been at work on the imaginations of those who have met or found traces of the bigfoot. In most cases we can usually dismiss the chances of deliberate hoaxing, if only because so many witnesses seem genuinely disturbed by their encounter – some to the extent of declaring they wished it had never happened, others being hurt or astonished at the amount of mockery and disbelief to which they have been subjected.

That leaves us with the possibility that the sightings or the traces were evidence of something else – something more familiar. Certainly it's hard to be sure that large footprint-like dents in the snow high in the mountains are actually footprints. A mountain goat will make quite tiny prints that melt somewhat in the sun to form large plate-like depressions, which then re-freeze to give the impression that an unusually heavy animal has trampled by. And while it is possible that in the wilderness areas of the United States a hungry bear may be mistaken for something more like a human being at night or in shadow, in the fastnesses of Asia there is an even odder risk.

Part of the training for certain religious sects' involves sending adepts out into the more remote (and unpleasant) parts of the mountains. Skilled in techniques of meditation and bodily control these extraordinary men can remain in these extreme conditions, without very much clothing and with no food at all, for days at a time. And having no desire to be disturbed in their contemplation, they will do their best to stay out of sight of mountaineers or other kinds of passer-by – meanwhile leaving mysterious footprints behind them, or tantalising glimpses of themselves as they slip away amid the snow and ice and rocks. How many of these shy and ascetic men have been mistaken for weird unearthly creatures – the 'abominable snowmen' of legend – it is impossible to say. But it is certainly possible that such cases of mistaken identity *have* occurred.

What, on the other hand, of the famous and controversial film that was shot of a bigfoot in 1967? There are certainly some rather odd features about it, not least (to the determined sceptic at least) the fact that it was a dedicated bigfoot-hunter who shot the movie. (People don't howl with derision when someone comes up with the antidote to some grim disease, for which they may have been searching for years, but the assumption generally is that the evidence gathered by seekers after the strange is somehow invalid since their motives are self-serving in the first place). One possibility is not often mentioned in connection with this case: that it was not Roger Patterson who was the hoaxer, but the bigfoot. Or rather someone who, aware of Patterson's interest in this kind of big game, dressed in a gorilla suit and gave him a run for his money. On the other hand, he might just have got some footage of the real thing.

Perhaps oddest of all the tales that surround bigfeet are those concerning their involvement with UFOs: occasionally the mysterious man-beasts appear at the same time as weird lights in the night and sometimes have strange psychological effects on the witnesses.

## Winged things and werewolves

This may be some form of hallucination, or it may be some intrusion from a completely unexplained 'parallel reality', but it does make a connection, perhaps, with some of the more astounding stories of mysterious *flying* creatures, some of which bear no relation at all to conventional bird life – and precious little even to the wildest stretches of the human imagination. Whether these come from another dimension, or are just possibly material creations of the human mind that occur only in certain rare circumstances, or are something else altogether, one can only speculate. And it is after all no less possible that, if the lakes of Scotland, Ireland and North America are harbouring strange forms of marine life, the more remote areas of the country may be hiding the nests of equally peculiar winged creatures.

The thought that material reality as we understand it may occasionally become plastic, may be putty in the hands of the mind, does seem particularly appropriate when we ponder the bizarre and frightening history of the werewolf. Reported by the ancient Greeks thousands of years ago, and still heard of from time to time in the modern era, the werewolf phenomenon is one of the most gruesome and most perplexing of all unexplained animal manifestations. *Is* it a delusion? A superstition that is fostered by ignorance, tradition and fear? Or is there some interaction here between the mind and body that can bring such creatures into being, a curse to themselves and their victims alike?

These questions are all raised by the reports that follow in these pages – questions in their way no less strange than the animals that inspire them.

PETER BROOKESMITH

**Everyone has heard tales of the 'abominable snowman' – or yeti – of the Himalayas. But sightings of mysterious animals, neither man nor beast, have been reported from all over the world: from North America, China, Australia, Africa, the wastes of Siberia and the Amazon jungle. JANET and COLIN BORD sift the evidence, and present he case for the reality of these elusive creatures**

'WILD MEN OF THE WOODS' are common figures in folklore throughout the world. In medieval Britain they were known as 'wood-woses' or 'woodhouses', and can be seen depicted in carvings in East Anglian churches. Though it is tempting to dismiss wood-woses as colourful figments of the rural imagination, a recent stream of reports of sightings from the North American continent of 'man-beasts' up to 8 feet (2.4 metres) tall – make these not so easy to ignore.

Bigfoot – or sasquatch, to give it the Indian name that is used in the province of British Columbia in Canada – makes the headlines so frequently nowadays that similar sightings in more distant or less publicity-conscious parts of the world tend to be overlooked. Yet from time to time reports emerge from the Himalayas, traditionally thought of as the home of the yeti or abominable snowman, of strange footprints in the snow or, less frequently, distant sightings of what is taken to be the yeti itself. In 1974, a Nepalese girl guarding a herd of yaks 14,000

# Man, myth or monster?

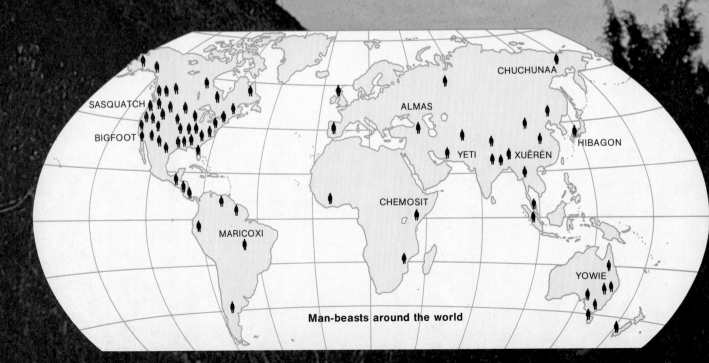

Man-beasts around the world

feet (4250 metres) up in the mountains near Mount Everest was attacked by a yeti and in 1978 Lord and Lady Hunt, revisiting Nepal to commemorate the 1953 ascent of Everest, saw and photographed large tracks in the snow around their huts.

Much has been written about the yeti over the years, although the number of actual sightings has been fairly small. In contrast, very little has been written about sightings of 'wild men' or 'man-beasts' in China, but from what has been published it seems they are fairly active in some remote areas. In the mid-1970s strange encounters with unknown creatures were reported from Hopeh and Shansi provinces – forested, mountainous country in northern China.

Particularly dramatic was the report made by 33-year-old Pang Gensheng, a commune leader, in June 1977. Pang was chopping wood in the Taibai Mountains of central Shansi province when he saw a 'hairy man':

It came closer and closer. I got scared and kept retreating until my back was against a stone cliff and I couldn't go any further. The hairy man came up to 7 or 8 feet [2.1 or 2.4 metres], and then to about 5 feet [1.5 metres] from me. I raised my axe, ready to fight for my life. We stood like that, neither of us moving, for more than an hour. Then I groped for a stone and threw it at him. It hit him in the chest. He uttered several howls and rubbed the spot with his left hand. Then he turned left and leaned against a tree, then walked away slowly toward the bottom of the gully. He kept making a mumbling sound.

The 'man' was about 7 feet (2.1 metres) tall, with a sloping forehead and deep-set black eyes. His jaw jutted out, and he had broad front teeth. Dark brown hair hung long and loose over his shoulders, and his body and face were covered with short hair. His long arms reached below his knees, and he walked upright with his legs wide apart.

Researchers at the Institute of Palaeo-anthropology and Vertebrate Palaeontology

Background picture: the Himalayas, home of the yeti, or abominable snowman

Below left: a footprint, allegedly of a yeti, found near Menlung Base of the 1951 Himalayan expedition. It is regarded as the best piece of photographic evidence for the existence of the yeti

Below right: in February 1980, a Polish climber took this photograph on Mount Everest at 16,000 feet (4800 metres). The footprint measures 14 inches (36 centimetres) long and 7 inches (17 centimetres) wide

of the 'wild men'. These mountains are a north-westerly extension of the Himalayas. In the summer of 1979 a Soviet expedition there found footprints $13\frac{1}{2}$ inches (34.3 centimetres long and $6\frac{1}{2}$ inches (16.5 centimetres) wide at the toes, but no one actually saw who or what made them.

'Man-beasts' have also been seen in Siberia, in the inhospitable northern territory of the Soviet Union. In the early 1960s a hunter living near the River Ob saw two such creatures when they came out of the forest one evening, while he was walking with his dogs. The dogs ran off in terror, but were not harmed. Dogs are usually frightened by these unknown monsters; in America bigfeet seem to dislike dogs and have been known to injure or even kill them. The Siberian hunter noted that the wild men were covered with dark hair, had long arms and turned their feet outwards when walking. Their eyes glowed dark red – yet another characteristic that indicates a similarity with bigfeet.

In the 1920s, a chuchunaa (a name meaning 'outcast' given to the man-beast in the Yakutiya region of eastern Siberia) was seen by villagers out berry-picking.

It was also picking berries and stuffing them into its mouth with both hands. On catching sight of us, he stood up to his full height. He was very tall and lean, over 2 metres [over 6 feet], they say Barefoot and dressed in deerskin, he had very long arms and a mop of unkempt hair. His face was as big as a human's. His forehead was small and

of the Chinese Academy of Sciences have been investigating such reports, but so far have not been able to solve the riddle of the 'wild man'. Even so, it it significant that the detailed description given by Pang Gensheng is similar to those given by witnesses elsewhere in the world. And the creature's behaviour is quite typical.

## Footprints in the snow

Research and investigation have also been undertaken in the Soviet Union, where Dr Jeanna Kofman has been on the trail of the so-called 'almas' in the Caucasus Mountains since 1955. She has received many eye-witness reports and has personally interviewed about 4000 people.

One of them was 39-year-old Mukhamed Tomakov, a farm manager, who in 1946 caught an almas in a mountain hut at Getmish. The creature was man-like, but covered with hair, and ran on all fours, standing on its hind legs whenever it stopped. (Sometimes, but not often, American bigfeet have been seen running on all fours.) Once the creature was safely inside the hut, Tomakov latched the door and went to get a rope. When he returned the door was open and the hut empty.

The Pamir Mountains on the southern border of the Soviet Union are another haunt

Above: the carved figure of a woodwose in the porch of Peasenhall Church, Suffolk. Woodwoses, or 'wild men of the woods', are said to have inhabited England in the Middle Ages, but they have apparently become extinct with the gradual spread of towns and villages

Right: a line of footprints said to have been made by a yeti. An alternative explanation, however, is that they were made by a mountain goat. The sun then melted the snow around the hoof marks, enlarging them

protruded over his eyes like the peak of a cap. His chin was large and broad, far bigger than a human's. Other than being a little taller, he was very much like a human. The next moment he ran away. He ran very fast, leaping high after every third step.

In America, too, bigfeet have been seen eating berries, and there have even been occasional reports of them actually wearing clothing.

## 'X' marks the spot

All continents still have some areas of wilderness, jungles or forested mountains that are rarely penetrated by outsiders. (Europe has the smallest area of uncivilised territory, which may explain why man-beast reports are almost non-existent there.) Vast tracts of unexplored land may conceal all manner of unknown creatures, not just wild men or man-beasts. In the East, man-beasts have been reported in Malaysia, where there is still plenty of jungle to conceal anything that wishes to stay hidden. Of course, the more remote the country, the less likely outsiders are to hear about unexpected encounters with these unknown life forms, unless expeditions are mounted with the intention of tracking them down.

This explains why we have only fragmentary data from South America and Africa. Yet what we do hear suggests there is plenty of activity. In 1978 Jacqueline Roumeguere Eberhardt of the Centre Nationale de la Recherche Scientifique in Paris published information on her research into the African man-beast, which she has somewhat unimaginatively named 'X'. At that time she had 31 accounts of sightings in 11 Kenyan forests, and she was able to identify four separate types of 'X'. One native was captured and carefully examined by an 'X' before being pushed away in the direction of his home.

Reports sometimes surface from far less promising areas. Our western image of Japan as a small, industrial nation leaves little room for remote uninhabited country able to support a population of man-beasts. Yet in the early 1970s there were several sightings of the Hibagon (as the beast became known) on Mount Hiba near Hiroshima. Farmer Albert Kubo saw this 5-foot (1.5-metre), big-eyed, smelly creature in 1974 when he was out in his rice fields spreading fertiliser. It was standing on a path, and Mr Kubo began to approach it before he realised what it was.

He said: 'I was petrified, but the stench was what really got me. He must have bathed in a septic tank and dried off with cow dung. I nearly passed out. Luckily enough, though, I managed to turn and run before it realised I was there. I ran 5 miles (8 kilometres) straight home without ever looking back over my shoulder.' The strong smell of many North American bigfeet is often described by witnesses in equally graphic terms.

The continent of Australia has many thousands of square miles of territory rarely visited by man and, as might be expected, it too has its man-beast. The Aborigines, who were apparently well aware of its existence,

## Is this the yeti?

One of the most popular explanations of the yeti's origins is that it is descended from the giant ape *Gigantopithecus*, whose fossilised remains have been found in India and China. Examination of the fossils indicates that *Gigantopithecus* lived between 12 million and 500,000 years ago. Also during this period, the Himalayas were rising by as much as 8000 to 10,000 feet (2500 to 3000 metres). Because of this increase in height of the mountains, many species of animals, including the yeti's ancestor, may have become isolated.

Some experts argue that though the yeti's footprints have been discovered above the snowline (a bare terrain that is unable to support a large mammal) its present home is actually lower down in the forested valleys. Here, vegetation is dense, fog is common and there are few human inhabitants to disturb the yeti. But, as a result of seasonal changes, they must sometimes cross the high snow passes to reach nearby valleys – and leave those telltale footprints.

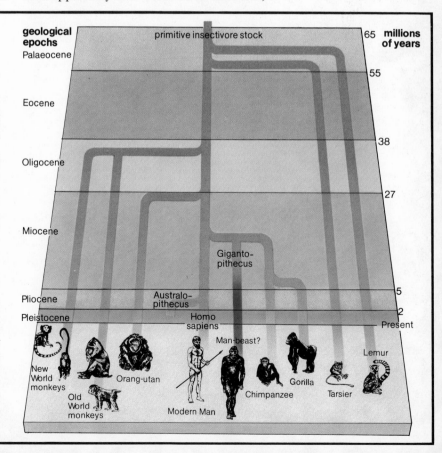

gave it many different names, but today it is usually called the yowie. Sightings have been regularly reported, especially in New South Wales and Queensland, since the late 18th century. On 3 October 1894 a boy named Johnnie McWilliams saw one while he was riding from his home at Snowball to the Jinden Post Office in New South Wales.

'A big man covered with long hair' suddenly appeared from behind a tree and seems to have been as surprised at the encounter as was the young Johnnie, for he ran off across open country, knocking his foot against a log and crying out in pain. He kept looking back as he ran, until he went out of sight over a low hill. The 'man' was over 6 feet (1.8 metres) tall and heavily built.

Joseph and William Webb, preparing to camp out one night at the turn of the century in the ranges of Brindabella, New South Wales, had a rather more dramatic encounter with a yowie. They heard a 'deep guttural bellowing' and noises, as if something was crashing through the scrub. According to John Gale, founder and editor of *The Queanbeyan Age*, writing in his book *An Alpine excursion* (1903):

Next moment a thing appeared walking erect, though they saw only its head and shoulders. It was hirsute, so much of the creature as was visible, and its head was set so deep between its shoulders that it was scarcely perceptible. It was approaching towards their camp. Now it was in full view, and was of the stature of a man. moving with long strides and a heavy tramp. It was challenged: 'Who are you? Speak, or we'll fire'. Not an intelligible word came in response; only the guttural bellowing. Aim was taken; the crack of a rifle rang out along the gully; but the

thing, if hit, was not disabled; for at the sound of the shot it turned and fled.

That the men saw no evidence of the bullet having struck its target does not necessarily mean that they missed. There is some evidence from North America that ordinary guns are useless against the hairy giants, either because they are not powerful enough, or for some stranger reason.

Australian yowie researcher Rex Gilroy has collected more than 3000 sighting reports and, as in North America, there was a big increase in reports during the 1970s. A particularly close sighting, where the witness was able to get a good look at a yowie of 7 feet (2.1 metres), was reported by a National Parks worker in the Springbrook area of Queensland in March 1978. Hearing a grunting sound, he thought a pig was loose and went into the forest to look for it.

Then something made me look up and there, about 12 feet [3.7 metres] in front of me, was this big black hairy man-thing. It looked more like a gorilla than anything. It had huge hands and one of them was wrapped round a sapling.

It had a flat, black shiny face, with two big yellow eyes and a hole for a mouth. It just stared at me and I stared back. I was so numb I couldn't even raise the axe I had in my hand. We seemed to stand there staring at each other for about 10 minutes before it suddenly gave off a foul smell that made me vomit – then it just made off sideways and disappeared.

Both its appearance and behaviour suggest that the yowie is a close cousin to the North American bigfoot.

Left: music teacher Richard Brown stands beside the fence near The Dalles, Oregon, where he saw a bigfoot in 1971. He followed the bigfoot's movements through the telescopic sights of his rifle

Below: Igor Bourtsev, a Russian 'snowman' hunter, holding a cast of a footprint found on 21 August 1979 in the Gissar Range of the Pamir-Alai Mountains, Tadzhikistan, in central Asia. The footprint, believed to have been made by an almas, measures 13.5 inches (34 centimetres) long and 6.5 inches (16 centimetres) wide at the toes. It is very nearly the same size as 'yeti' footprints found in the Himalayas

# On the Bigfoot trail

**Hundreds of sightings all over the North American continent suggest that the fabled bigfoot really does exist. But how can this primitive creature survive in the world's most developed society?**

RELIABLE REPORTS OF 'man-beasts' on the North American continent have been traced as far back as the 1830s. We have to rely on old newspaper accounts for our data before 1900, but determined researchers have found some intriguing descriptions of beasts very similar to those reported today. For example, in 1851 a local newspaper carried the story of two hunters in Greene County, Arkansas, who saw a herd of cattle being chased by 'an animal bearing the unmistakable likeness of humanity'.

He was of gigantic stature, the body being covered with hair and the head with long locks that fairly enveloped the neck and shoulders. The 'wild man', after looking at them deliberately for a short time, turned and ran away with great speed, leaping 12 to 14 feet [3.6 to 4.3 metres] at a time. His footprints measured 13 inches [33 centimetres] each.

The newspaper reporter added that the beast was thought to be 'a survivor of the earthquake disaster which desolated that region in 1811'. In nearly all these early reports the man-beasts are referred to as 'wild men', the assumption being that they must be humans who have taken to the woods and in so doing somehow developed a thick coat of body hair. Modern evolutionary theory, however, suggests that this is unlikely.

The location of the 1851 sighting in Arkansas shows that bigfoot reports are not confined to the north-western states (northern California, Oregon and Washington) and British Columbia, where so many originate. Although these areas, with their vast tracts of forested mountains, have produced more reports than other regions, bigfeet or their footprints have been seen in nearly all the American states and Canadian provinces. Florida, far away from what is thought of as traditional bigfoot territory, has been particularly rich in sightings of the similar 'skunk ape' in recent years.

Many reports simply describe a man-beast, seen briefly in wooded country. But there are enough detailed reports for trends and characteristics to be apparent. Bigfeet seem to be timid, not wishing to get too close to humans. However, they also have a streak of curiosity and sometimes come close to people camping in the woods at night, look through their belongings, and occasionally also rock their camper or car. This behaviour, and early reports of the destruction of mineral prospectors' camps, may suggest a wish to frighten intruders away.

Bigfeet have also been seen wandering near rural houses and settlements, possibly attracted by the easy availability of food in such places. But despite their frightening appearance and the provocative behaviour of their discoverers, (whose reaction is frequently to shoot first and ask questions afterwards), bigfeet are not aggressive towards humans. Reports of injuries caused by them are rare.

As the 20th century progressed and more people became aware of bigfeet, so more reports came in concerning old as well as

Above and over: Five stills from the only cine film ever taken of a bigfoot at Bluff Creek, California, in 1967. Rigorous analysis has not proved the film to be a fake – but sceptics still insist that the creature is a large actor dressed in animal skins. Casts (below) were taken of footprints found in the area after the sighting

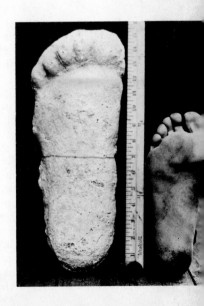

recent sightings, until in the 1960s and 1970s there was a vast number of reports on file. Although this was obviously due in part to the greater publicity, did it also mean that bigfeet were being seen more frequently? Since their habitat must gradually be shrinking as civilisation advances, it would be reasonable to expect their numbers to be declining. Perhaps it is this very pressure on living space that forces them to visit settlements for food and this might explain the increased number of reported sightings.

The *Bigfoot casebook* records nearly 1000 sightings in the past 150 years and this collection of cases is by no means complete. If, as has been estimated, only about one tenth of all sightings are ever reported, then there may have been as many as 10,000 sightings during that period. There are also many other reports of large, human-like footprints being found, usually in mud, snow or sand where they show up well, and it is usually assumed that a bigfoot left these tracks, even when the creature has not been

a very large man-like creature about 6½ or 7 feet [2 or 2.1 metres] tall came into view.

It was walking on its hind legs, was covered with dark hair, had a bearded face and large chest and so far as I could see was not wearing clothes of any kind. Startled, I let out a yell of alarm and the creature instantly turned and ran off into the woods, still on its hind legs. I told some of my co-workers about it and some laughed but others said they, too, had seen it. No one had an explanation for it and no name was given to it, but all agreed that it was a large ape-like something and that it also resembled a very large man.

### Kidnapped by a man-beast

Another bigfoot report, dating from 1924, describes what, if it is true, is the most dramatic bigfoot encounter on record. Albert Ostman claims to have been kidnapped by a bigfoot and held captive for several days

Top: prospector Albert Ostman claimed to have been held captive by a bigfoot family in British Columbia in 1924

seen. Sometimes researchers investigating reports also find hair and faeces that are suspected to be a bigfoot's, but analyses done on these substances are usually irritatingly inconclusive.

A selection of a few of the many sightings reported this century will give a clear picture of bigfoot and his behaviour. In 1969 Albert M. Fletcher wrote about his encounter 50 years before, when he was a lumber-camp worker in Washington.

In the fall of 1917 when I was 17 years old I was working for a lumber camp on the Cowlitz River in the state of Washington. One moonlit evening I was walking down a logging road en route to a dance when I had the uneasy feeling that something was following close behind me. I kept looking over my shoulder but could not see anything. When I came to a bend in the road I ducked behind a tree and waited to see what it was. Almost immediately

before he managed to escape. The kidnap took place near Toba Inlet in British Columbia, when Ostman was prospecting and camping in the mountains. An 8-foot (2.4-metres) bigfoot picked him up in his sleeping bag one night and carried him across country for what seemed to the hot and cramped captive like three hours.

It was still dark when they arrived at their destination, but when it got light Ostman saw there were four bigfeet, male and female adults and male and female children. During his captivity Ostman was able to study the family's way of life, and to ponder his best method of escape. All attempts were blocked by the 'old man', as Ostman called him, whose mere size was an imposing deterrent. Ostman had his rifle with him but was loth to cause the creatures any injury, since they had not harmed him. He finally escaped by feeding the 'old man' a huge quantity of snuff and thereby incapacitating him. While the bigfoot rushed to find some water, Ostman grabbed his belongings and ran for his life.

Encounters in which the witness is able to get a long, close look at the creature are the most interesting; a perceptive and unflurried witness can add greatly to our knowledge of the creature. One of the best reports of this kind was made by William Roe, who saw a bigfoot on Mica Mountain in British Columbia in October 1955.

Roe was hidden in a bush, so the bigfoot, a female about 6 feet (1.8 metres) tall and 3 feet (1 metre) wide and weighing around 300 pounds (135 kilograms), came towards him unaware she was being watched. When the bigfoot was 20 feet (6 metres) away, she squatted by the bush Roe was hiding in.

He later wrote a careful description of the bigfoot's head, face and hair, of the shape of her body and the way she walked. He wondered briefly if he had unknowingly stepped into a film set and was looking at a made-up actor, but soon discarded that idea. His report continues:

Finally, the wild thing must have got my scent, for it looked directly at me through an opening in the bush. A look of amazement crossed its face. It looked so comical at that moment I had to grin. Still in a crouched position, it backed up three or four short steps, then straightened up to its full height and started to walk rapidly back the way it had come. For a moment it watched me over its shoulder as it went, not exactly afraid, but as though it wanted no contact with anything strange.

Roe considered shooting what would be a unique specimen, and even raised his rifle. But he could not fire. 'Although I have called the creature "it", I felt now that it was a human being and I knew I would never forgive myself if I killed it.'

Human or animal? The witnesses are not sure, and neither are the researchers. 'If only we had a corpse to examine,' they cry. But those who feel that the priority is to kill a bigfoot and thus prove its existence once and for all are opposed by those who feel equally strongly that the creature should be left in peace. What gives man the right to commit murder simply to satisfy his curiosity?

A few reports suggest that someone with enough patience and nerve might even be able to make friends with a bigfoot. In the autumn of 1966 a couple living near Lower Bank in New Jersey found footprints 17 inches (43 centimetres) long outside their house, and saw a face peering in at a window over 7 feet (2.1 metres) high. They regularly left vegetable scraps for the bigfoot, which it ate, but one night they left nothing and their visitor showed its annoyance by throwing a dustbin against the wall. A shot fired into the air failed to deter it, so the man fired *at* the bigfoot, which ran away and did not return.

Thirty feet (9-metres) of wobbly 16-millimetre colour film shook the bigfoot-hunting world in 1967, and the questions posed by the film still have not been answered to everyone's satisfaction. Behind the camera was bigfoot-hunter Roger Patterson, who in October that year was riding through the remote forests of the Bluff Creek area of northern California with Bob Gimlin, on the lookout for signs of bigfeet. Their horses reared in fright when they suddenly came across a female bigfoot squatting beside a creek. Patterson leapt down, grabbed his camera and began to run after the retreating figure, filming as he went. Before the bigfoot was lost to sight among the trees, it turned to look back at the men. The famous strip of film has been analysed many times since 1967, but although no one has been able to prove it a hoax, scientists remain suspicious.

This may be due to natural caution, or the curious argument that 'Bigfoot can't exist, therefore it doesn't'. Meanwhile this creature continues to appear regularly in North America, to alarm but not hurt the witnesses who are invariably taken by surprise, and to puzzle all who ponder its presence.

Bigfoot hunter Rene Dahinden stands beside a statue of a bigfoot, sculpted by Jim McClarin, at Willow Creek, California. The figure, modelled on descriptions of bigfeet seen in the area, is 8 feet (2.4 metres) tall, 41 inches (1.04 metres) wide at the shoulder and has feet measuring 18 by 10 inches (46 by 25 centimetres)

# Creatures from the void?

**Some man-beasts seem to be impervious to bullets, while others appear to be able to vanish at will. What are these strange and terrifying creatures?**

THE BIGFOOT RIDDLE is not an easy one to solve. It is not simply a question of ascertaining whether or not the creature exists and, if it does, whether it is human or animal. Some reports, especially the more recent ones, have features that seem to deepen the mystery.

The average height of a bigfoot seems to be between 6 and 7 feet (1.8 and 2.1 metres), though much smaller ones are sometimes reported; these could be youngsters. However, much taller ones are occasionally reported. A 15-foot (4.5-metre) creature was seen by a USAF Staff Sergeant and two friends while they were camping at Belt Creek Canyon, Montana, in August 1977. They shot at it, but turned tail and drove away in their cars when it began to run towards them. Reports of fleeting sightings of this sort,

Above: an alleged yeti scalp belonging to the Buddhist Pangboche monastery in the Himalayas of Nepal. Despite all the efforts of hunters, no unquestionably genuine yeti remains have been made available for research

Right: 16-year-old Tim Meissner (left) estimates the height of a bigfoot he saw and shot at near his home in British Columbia, Canada, in April 1979. The creature, about 9 feet (2.7 metres) tall, was standing beside this tree when Tim saw it

however, can never be taken at face value: size, for instance, is easily mistaken under conditions of stress.

Sometimes, however, an accurate calculation of height can be made. In April 1979, 16-year-old Tim Meissner saw a bigfoot twice in three days near his rural home in British Columbia. The first time, while fishing with friends at Dunn Lake near Barriere, he heard a high-pitched screech and saw on the lake's far shore a bigfoot with its arms raised. It ran away as the youths went to investigate. Hidden under branches and moss they found a deer with a broken neck.

Two days later, Tim Meissner returned with four friends, armed with a gun. They split up to search for the bigfoot. By an astonishing stroke of luck, Meissner saw it again. His first reaction was to shoot at the tall, black, hairy creature with glaring bright eyes and shoulders 4 feet (1.2 metres) wide. He seems to have hit it, since it went down on one knee, but then it got up and ran away at great speed. When Tim saw the bigfoot it was about 50 yards (45 metres) away, standing beside a tree. Later he returned to the tree and was able to estimate that the creature he had seen was about 9 feet (2.7 metres) tall.

## The mystery deepens

Some bigfeet smell revolting. During a flurry of sightings around Little Eagle, South Dakota, in the autumn of 1977, one witness reported: 'It was like a stink of a dead person, long dead. It stayed in the air for maybe 10 to 15 minutes afterwards.' But by no means all bigfeet smell bad. It has been suggested, for example, that they can release the smell at will, perhaps to ensure that people keep their distance. Another strange feature is that some bigfeet have exceptionally large eyes which seem, uncannily, to glow. They are

usually red, but sometimes yellow or green.

The footprint evidence is also puzzling. Five-toed prints are most commonly found, resembling large human feet. But sometimes the prints appear to have only two toes, or three, four or sometimes six. Perhaps this anomaly is explicable in terms of over-eager investigators misinterpreting less than perfect footprints.

A significant number of reports, many of them made by experienced huntsmen, tell of a disturbing phenomenon: some bigfeet are apparently completely unharmed by bullets.

There seem to be three possible explanations: the guns used are just not powerful

number of other cases in which UFOS and bigfeet are reported as having been seen at the same time and in the same area. Coincidence? Or are they both part of the same phenomenon?

Another strange case involving a UFO took place on a farm near Greensburg, Pennsylvania, on the evening of 25 October 1973. When a large, bright red luminous ball was seen to come down in a field a 22-year-old farmer's son, pseudonym Stephen, went to investigate. He and two 10-year-old boys he took with him saw the shining object on or close to the ground. They also saw, near the ball, two tall, ape-like creatures with green

Left: these bones are claimed by the monks of Pangboche monastery to be the skeletal hand of a yeti. Although the hand seems small in comparison with the scalp (opposite), the remains can be taken as evidence to support the theory that the yeti is a form of ape – the hands of many ape species are relatively small

enough to tackle such a creature, or the witness in his excitement did not aim properly (although some shots were fired from very close range) – or bigfeet are not made of flesh and blood.

## Bigfeet and UFOS?

If the theory that bigfeet are not composed of flesh and blood sounds incredible, there is some even more extraordinary evidence that tends to support it: the claim that some bigfeet are apparently able to disappear or dematerialise. A Pennsylvanian woman, confronted by one on her doorstep one night in February 1974, shot into its middle from a distance of 6 feet (1.8 metres). She was astounded to see it disappear in a flash of light! Other eye-witnesses have reported signs of insubstantiality in the bigfeet they have seen.

In the Pennsylvania case the witness's son-in-law, who came to help on hearing the shot, saw other bigfeet at the edge of nearby woods. He also saw a bright red flashing light hovering over the woods. There are a

glowing eyes and long, dark hair. The creatures began to approach them.

Stephen fired over their heads, but they kept walking towards the witnesses. So he fired three rounds straight into the largest creature, which raised its hand. The UFO disappeared and the bigfeet turned and slowly walked into the nearby woods.

Investigators were immediately called in, and although they saw neither UFO nor bigfeet, they found a glowing area where the UFO had been. Stephen subsequently went into a trance.

## Rival killers

Bigfoot cases with such bizarre details are by no means widespread. They are generally reported in states far away from the traditional bigfoot territory in the north west of the continent. Some of the veteran bigfoot hunters and investigators are sceptical of apparent paranormal cases, possibly feeling that they do not wish to become involved in fringe eccentricities.

Those hunters who feel it is now their

life's work to convince the world of the existence of the bigfoot have a hard task for, despite the mass of data, few professional scientists or anthropologists will give their work a second glance. Certainly, if a bigfoot corpse was obtained, their case would, of course, be incontrovertible. Consequently there is rivalry – even open hostility – among those hunters who compete to be first to capture or kill one. So far they have been totally unsuccessful.

Even the rare cases of killed or captured man-beasts have not resulted in any corpses being made available for study. In 1917 Swiss geologist Francois de Loys shot a 5-foot (1.5-metre) animal on the borders of Columbia and Venezuela, which zoologist Dr Bernard Heuvelmans believes may have been an unknown type of spider monkey.

Of many reports from the USSR, the most recent tells of a man-beast captured and later killed in the mountains near Buinaksk in Daghestan. A Soviet army officer, Colonel Karapetyan, saw the creature while it was still alive and later remembered it vividly:

Above: this 'man-beast' was shot by Swiss geologist Francois de Loys on the borders of Columbia and Venezuela in 1917. It is now thought it may have been a kind of spider monkey

Above right: a drawing of the hairy man-beast captured and killed near Buinaksk in Daghestan, USSR, in 1941. The creature was seen alive by Colonel V. S. Karapetyan (right) but was never made available for scientific research

I can still see the creature as it stood before me, a male, naked and barefooted. And it was doubtlessly a man, because its entire shape was human. The chest, back, and shoulders, however, were covered with shaggy hair of a dark brown colour . . . his height was above average – about 180 centimetres [6 feet]. He stood before me like a giant, his mighty chest thrust forward. . . His eyes told me nothing. They were dull and empty – the eyes of an animal. And he seemed to me like an animal and nothing more . . . this was no disguised person, but a wild man of some kind.

In December 1968 came a report from Minnesota, USA, of a bigfoot corpse frozen in a block of ice, Dr Heuvelmans and biologist Ivan T. Sanderson saw it and, despite the difficulties of examination, were convinced that the ice contained the fresh corpse of a hitherto unknown form of hominid. For various complex reasons, however, the corpse was never made available for proper examination.

There are several reasons why, despite the number of sightings, hunters are not able simply to go into the forest and kill a bigfoot. Bigfeet are reputed to possess intimate knowledge of the terrain they inhabit such that they can travel through it far quicker than a man and remain completely concealed. Given these alleged characteristics the prospect for the hunter of capturing or killing one remains remote.

Most of the time, all the intrepid bigfoot hunter can do is interview witnesses, examine footprints, and collect newspaper reports. Such work, carried out by dedicated enthusiasts all over the North American continent, has resulted in an accumulation of data and many intriguing theories about the nature of bigfeet – and indeed all man-beasts. Nevertheless, without high-quality photographs, a corpse or a skeleton, or even part of one, all that scientists can do is speculate about possible explanations.

## Man, beast . . . or hologram?

All we know for certain is that large, human-like footprints have been found in large numbers in remote areas – and not all of them are likely to be fakes – and that well over 1000 people in North America alone have reported seeing tall, hairy man-beasts. The various theories that have been put forward to explain these facts apply equally well to man-beasts seen all over the world.

On the negative side, it has been suggested that all man-beast reports are hoaxes. This seems unlikely. Another suggestion is that people may be misidentifying known animals under poor viewing conditions. This explanation could account for some of the sightings, but by no means all of them. Yet another view is that it is simply a case of hallucination. People who have seen too many horror films have had hallucinations –

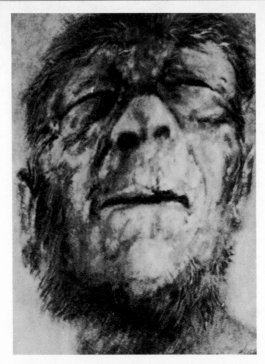

and claim to have seen something that simply is not there. May not man-beast sightings be a similar case? Such a theory does not, however, account for the footprints, which appear to be real enough.

A more sympathetic view is that the man-beasts may be some form of giant ape or perhaps an early form of man-like ape, *Gigantopithecus*. This seems possible, even likely in some parts of the world. Alternatively, man-beasts may really be men, prehistoric survivals that have managed to stay concealed against all the odds.

Some people have argued that man-beasts are some kind of paranormal phenomenon. They may come into being when certain types of energy are available (electrical, nuclear or psychic, for example). Bigfeet have sometimes been reported near energy sources. An even more remote possibility is that man-beasts come from UFOs, for reasons as yet unknown. Against this, it has been pointed out that if UFOs and man-beasts are both paranormal phenomena, they are just as likely to have been formed in the same way – which may explain why they sometimes appear close together in time and space. Finally, man-beasts could be holograms, three-dimensional images projected from space by an unknown intelligence. If so, who or what is doing it – and why?

Investigators differ in their interpretations of the data, and perhaps no one explanation can account for all the reported sightings. It is most likely that the term 'man-beasts' covers a wide range of phenomena that, for unknown reasons, appear – or seem to appear – in similar guises. Whatever the truth may be, the man-beast phenomenon is an extraordinary and complex one that requires a great deal more research before any firm conclusions can be drawn.

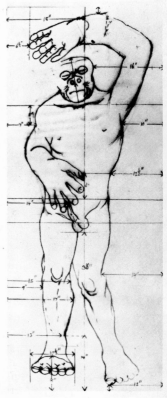

Left and below: sketches by biologist Ivan T. Sanderson of 'Bozo', a hairy man-beast seen frozen in a block of ice in Minnesota, USA, in December 1968. The owner apparently later replaced the corpse with a model – leaving only the evidence of Sanderson and zoologist Dr Bernard Heuvelmans, who had seen the original body, to prove it had ever existed

## Weird Winged Creatures

**Age-old myths tell of great birds that preyed upon human beings. Ornithologists scoff at the idea that such creatures exist in reality but, as JANET and COLIN BORD explain, some people think they have encountered such monsters – and some have felt the strength of their claws**

IN TIPPAH COUNTY, MISSOURI, USA, a teacher had this tragic story to tell in 1878:

A sad casualty occurred at my school a few days ago. The eagles have been very troublesome in the neighbourhood for some time past, carrying off pigs, lambs, etc. No one thought that they would attempt to prey upon children; but on Thursday, at recess, the little boys were out some distance from the house, playing marbles, when their sport was interrupted by a large eagle sweeping down and picking up little Jemmie Kenney, a boy of eight years, and flying away with him. The children cried out, and when I got out of the

# Monsters on the wing

house the eagle was so high that I could just hear the child screaming. The alarm was given, and from screaming and shouting in the air, etc., the eagle was induced to drop his victim; but his talons had been buried in him so deeply, and the fall was so great, that he was killed. . . .

This is not the only case of a child being carried away by an eagle. In 1838, in the mountains of Switzerland, a five-year-old girl called Marie Delex was snatched away from her friends. She was not carried to the bird's nest – a search party found two eaglets there, with heaps of goat and sheep bones, but no sign of her. It was not until two months had passed that a shepherd found her mutilated corpse, lying on a rock.

Svanhild Hantvigsen, a Norwegian, claims that when she was three years old, in 1932, she was seized by an eagle and carried to its nest. She was rescued by some people who had noticed the eagle's strange behaviour and she was lucky enough to escape without a scratch, though her dress was torn.

Such attacks are frightening, but not mysterious. Sometimes, however, there are reports of a different kind – of monstrous winged creatures that do not seem to fit the description of any bird known to ornithology. Sometimes they seem most like giant flying creatures that became extinct millions of years ago. And sometimes, as we shall see in a later article, they seem half human.

The largest living bird known to science is

the wandering albatross, which is seen only in the southern oceans and has the largest known wingspan – 11 feet (3.3 metres). Very close to it in size is the Andean condor, with a 10-foot (3-metre) wingspan. The Californian condor's wings span 9 feet (2.7 metres) – but it is thought that today less than 40 of these birds survive.

Left: five-year-old Marie Delex was borne away by a large bird in 1838. Local people assumed it was an eagle – yet scientists believe eagles are capable of lifting nothing heavier than a fawn or goat kid

Below left: Svanhild Hantvigsen displays the torn dress that she was wearing in 1932 when an eagle swooped on her and carried her to its nest. The arrival of rescuers saved her from the fate suffered by Marie Delex nearly 100 years before

Below: the dog belonging to Peter Swadley, a bear hunter, attempted to fight off an eagle that attacked his master in West Virginia, USA, in 1895. The dog was carried off, while Swadley was left badly injured

Even a condor would look tiny, however, alongside the teratorn, a bird that became extinct about 10,000 years ago. It is thought to have been the largest bird that has ever lived on Earth, having a length of 11 feet (3.3 metres), a wingspan of 25 feet (7.5 metres), and a weight of 160 to 170 pounds (72 to 76 kilograms). Fossils have been found in Argentina, Mexico and the southern United States; some of them are thought to be 5 to 8 million years old.

Huge birds figure in mythology. The Illini Indians painted a picture of a monstrous bird, the *piasa* or 'bird that devours men', on a rock face overlooking a river near Alton in Illinois. They used to fire bows or guns at the picture as they passed by in their canoes. The painting was seen by missionary explorers in the 17th century, before the rock face was destroyed. In the 1970s a new *piasa* design, following the traditional one, was repainted at Norman's Landing.

According to the Illini, the *piasa* is scaly, with a long tail, horns and red eyes. It can be seen once a year, at dawn on the first day of autumn, as it emerges from the river to pick a cave for the winter. But despite vigils by

students on bluffs above the Mississippi River, no one has seen the dreaded *piasa* in recent years.

However, some Indians claim to see another huge creature, the thunderbird, today. According to James Red Sky, an Ojibwa Indian from the Thunder Bay region of Ontario, Canada: 'We saw a thunderbird a few summers ago. A huge bird it was; a lot bigger than planes you see go by today. It didn't flap its wings. Not even once. It was white on the underside, black on top.'

Modern reports of giant birds in the USA began in the late 19th century. At Dent's Run, Pennsylvania, in 1882, one Fred Murray saw a flock of birds that, he said, looked like giant buzzards, with wingspans of more than 16 feet (5 metres).

In February 1895 the disappearance of 10-year-old Landy Junkins in Webster County, West Virginia, was ascribed to a giant bird. Landy was sent by her mother to a neighbour's house, but never arrived. A search party found her tracks in the snow: they left the path and went a few feet into a field. There, a number of tracks were crowded together, as if she had turned round and

Above: a carved human face peers out from a mask of a thunderbird, made by Haida Indians of the American north-west coast. The Haida believe that a human spirit can take on a thunderbird's form: this is symbolised by the closing of the mask's jaws

Above right: the *piasa*, a gigantic legendary bird, was shown in these rock paintings, which formerly existed near Alton, Illinois, USA. The bird terrorised the Illini Indians until the great chief Ouatogo offered himself as bait, while 20 warriors hid nearby. The bird was killed by their arrows, while Ouatogo was unharmed. The paintings commemorated the event

round, perhaps trying to avoid something. No trace of Landy was ever found.

An incident a few days later suggested what had happened to her. A bear hunter, Peter Swadley, was attacked by a massive bird, which swooped down and dug its talons in his back. Swadley was saved from death by his dog, which made for the bird. The bird turned its attention to the dog, ripping open its stomach with one stroke of its claws before flying off with the unfortunate animal. A deputy sheriff and his son also saw the giant 'eagle', which captured a fawn while they were in the forest hunting deer. They said the bird had a wingspan of 15 to 18 feet (4.5 to 5.5 metres), and a body as large as a man's.

The same monster was also thought to be responsible for the strange disappearance of a sheep from a locked shed. One morning,

Hanse Hardrick found one sheep missing, with a hole in the shed roof showing how it had been extracted.

Some eagle – able to carry away a fawn, a hunting dog, a sheep and a 10-year-old girl, and make a bold attempt to carry off a fully grown man!

Around 1940, in Pennsylvania, an author and local historian, Robert Lyman, was in the Black Forest near Coudersport, when he saw a brownish bird standing in the middle of a road. It stood 3 to 4 feet (about 1 metre) tall and had a short neck and short legs. When it flew off, Mr Lyman saw that its narrow wings, when extended, reached across the road – a span of 20 to 25 feet (6 to 7.5 metres). He wondered how such a big bird could fly through dense trees so easily.

In 1947 farmers around Ramore in Ontario, Canada, were experiencing problems with a giant black bird that was attacking their livestock. It had a hooked beak, huge talons, and yellow eyes 'the size of silver dollars'. A few months later an outbreak of sightings of big birds occurred in Illinois. 'There's a bird outside as big as a B-29!' gasped 12-year-old James Trares as he rushed indoors to his mother. That was in January 1948, and James was the first to report seeing the monster. He lived in Glendale, Illinois, and the bird he saw, wings flapping as it flew over, was grey-green in colour.

A former army colonel, Walter Siegmund, saw something similar on 4 April. He estimated that it was 4000 feet (1200 metres) up, and from his military experience he was quite convinced that 'it could only be a bird of some tremendous size.'

More sightings followed, including some over St Louis, Missouri. Several witnesses at first believed they were seeing an aeroplane because of its size – until it began to flap its wings and to perform bird-like manoeuvres. Policemen and flying instructors were among

Above: the magnificent bald eagle of North America. Fish are its favourite prey, but it has been blamed for attacks on small animals and children

Right: the Californian condor, hideous when at rest, is majestic in flight, gliding effortlessly for long distances. One of the world's rarest birds, it can attain 9 feet (2.7 metres) in wingspan. It attacks living animals, though like other vultures it feeds mainly on carrion

Right: the imagined abduction of an Alpine peasant woman's child by an eagle. The artist entitled this picture, published in 1900, *The robber of the skies*

Left: one of the rarer hazards of the American West: in 1870 a golden eagle attacked a woman rider near the track of the Pacific Railroad and was beaten off only after severely wounding her

the witnesses. The last sighting seems to have been on 30 April 1948. Charles Dunn could hardly believe his eyes when he saw a bird 'about the size of a Piper Cub plane', flying at about 3000 feet (900 metres) and flapping its wings.

Little more was seen of monster birds for nearly two decades, although in 1957 a huge bird with a wingspan of 25 to 30 feet (7.5 to 9 metres) was seen flying at about 500 feet (150 metres) over Renovo, Pennsylvania. In 1966 there were reports from Utah, West Virginia, Ohio and Kentucky, only some of which could be explained as sightings of rare known species.

Then, in 1975, during an outbreak of mysterious deaths of animals in Puerto Rico, large birds resembling whitish condors or vultures were seen. On 26 March Juan Muñiz Feliciano, a workman, was attacked by 'a terrible greyish creature with lots of feathers, a long thick neck, bigger than a goose'.

At the end of July 1977, a big bird was seen trying to steal a young pig weighing 50 to 60 pounds (22 to 27 kilograms) near Delava, Illinois. The bird had a companion. Both resembled Californian condors and had 8-foot (2.5-metre) wingspans. But an ecologist at the University of Illinois commented that condors are rare, almost to the point of extinction, could not lift such a weight and

Right: 10-year-old Marlon Lowe, victim of an attack by a large bird in 1977, with his mother, whose cry startled the bird into dropping the boy. The incident occurred in Illinois, home of the legends of the *piasa*

Below: Juan Muñiz Feliciano, a Puerto Rican workman, fights off an attack by a 'terrible greyish creature' one night in 1975. At about this time, farm animals were being killed and mutilated in a manner reminiscent of cattle mutilation cases on the American mainland

anyway feed on dead animals, not live ones.

What was it, then, that tried to abduct 10-year-old Marlon Lowe from the garden of his home at Lawndale, Illinois, on 25 July? That bird, too, was accompanied by another, and the near-tragedy took place only a few days before the abortive pig-stealing, and 10 miles (16 kilometres) away. Marlon was playing hide-and-seek when at 8.10 p.m. one of the birds snatched him off the ground. Fortunately his mother was at hand. She saw Marlon's feet dangling in the air and screamed, and the bird dropped the boy before he had been lifted very high. Mrs Lowe was only 10 feet (3 metres) away from the birds, and afterwards recalled: 'I'll always remember how that huge thing was bending its white ringed neck, and seemed to be trying to peck at Marlon, as it was flying away.' She described the birds as 'very black' except for the white rings around their necks, which were 18 inches (45 centimetres) long. They had hooked bills 6 inches (15 centimetres) long, and a wingspan of at least 8 feet (2.5 metres). She estimated they would have stood $4\frac{1}{2}$ feet (1.3 metres) tall had they landed. Six people watched the birds fly off towards Kickapoo Creek where there is heavy underbrush and thick tree cover.

But for the bird's being startled by Mrs Lowe's screams, Marlon would probably have suffered the same fate as Marie Delex, Jemmie Kenney and Landy Junkins. As it was, the Lowes suffered in other ways. They were harassed by people leaving dead birds on the front porch, and by unpleasant notes and telephone calls. At school Marlon, nicknamed 'Bird Boy', had literally to fight off the taunts of his fellows. His red hair turned grey, and for a year the frightened boy refused to go out after night had fallen.

The flying creature 'as big as a man' that attacked Armando Grimaldo in Texas, USA, in 1976, Featherless, beakless and with large red eyes, it swooped on him from above. When he had made his escape he found that his clothes had been torn, though he was uninjured. This incident was the most terrifying of a wave of sightings in Texas early that year

# Flight across time?

**Terrified witnesses have told of winged creatures that strikingly resembled pterodactyls, supposedly extinct for over 60 million years**

AN AMAZING REPORT in a learned journal, *The Zoologist* for July 1868, describes what the writer had seen earlier the same year at Copiapó, in Chile:

Yesterday, at about five o'clock in the afternoon, when the daily labours in this mine were over, and all the workmen were together awaiting their supper, we saw coming through the air . . . a gigantic bird, which at first we took for one of the clouds then partially darkening the atmosphere, supposing it to have been separated from the rest by the wind. Its course was from north-west to south-east; its flight rapid and in a straight line. As it was passing a short distance above our heads we could mark the strange formation of its body. Its immense wings were clothed with a grayish plumage, its monstrous head was like that of a locust, its eyes were wide open and shone like burning coals; it seemed to be covered with something resembling the thick and stout bristles of a boar, while on its body, elongated like that of a serpent, we could only see brilliant scales, which clashed together with a metallic sound as the strange animal turned its body in its flight.

In some ways this report resembles those of the aeroplane-sized birds seen over Illinois, USA, in the spring of 1948. But the Chilean workmen were closer to their 'bird' when they saw it and were able afterwards to describe its rather strange appearance. Was it really a bird, or could it have been a flying reptile?

Perhaps this was nothing more than a journalistic hoax, as the 'thunderbird' reportedly killed near Tombstone, Arizona, in 1890 is strongly suspected to be. The details came from an article in the Tombstone *Epitaph* for 26 April 1890. What supposedly happened is briefly told. Two ranchers, riding in the desert, chased a winged monster 'resembling a huge alligator with an extremely elongated tail and an immense pair of wings', which was apparently exhausted. They got near enough to kill it with gunfire, and then set about measuring it. It was about 92 feet (28 metres) long, with a wingspan of some 160 feet (49 metres). The wings and body were without hair or feathers, and the jaw was full of sharp teeth. The whole Tombstone saga is complicated by the fact that a thunderbird was supposed to have been killed in the same area in 1886. There are researchers who claim to have seen a photograph of it, but so far no one has been able to locate this elusive picture. No one seems to know what happened to the corpse of the thunderbird, if it ever existed. Several good stories published in American newspapers during the second half of the 19th century have since been found to be tall tales, and this may be another.

If the Copiapó and Tombstone 'birds' really existed, they sound more like prehistoric monsters than the birds we are familiar with today. Some years earlier, in the 1850s, a French newspaper reported that a living pterodactyl had been discovered by men blasting rock at Culmont in Haute-Marne, France. The huge, hideous creature emerged from a cavity in the rock, and it looked like a bat the size of a large goose. It was black in colour, and its wingspan was about 10 feet (3 metres). Unfortunately, present-day researchers have been unable to find any supporting evidence for this story.

Nineteenth-century pterodactyl reports are admittedly unreliable, but the 20th century has produced some puzzling American accounts that are less easily dismissed. The earliest 20th-century reports concern an enigmatic monster, the so-called 'Jersey devil'.

In January 1909 this weird 'thing' terrorised the state of New Jersey. Its lair was

Right: pterodactyls appeared about 150 million years ago, and so were contemporary with the dinosaurs. They lived in flocks in coastal areas. Their jaws were equipped with powerful teeth, though they lived only on fish and insects. For 85 million years they flourished, and then supposedly died out – yet they fit many modern descriptions of strange flying creatures

Below: an enormous 'bird' seen by workmen at Copiapó, Chile, in 1868. The animal was a curious hybrid, since its wings were covered with feathers, while its body was covered with scales, which the watchers on the ground could hear clashing with a metallic sound

supposed to be somewhere in the Pine Barrens, an isolated area in the south-east of the state. All manner of strange phenomena were attributed to the Jersey devil over the years, but the events we are describing concern sightings of a strange winged monster and the footprints it left behind.

## Antics of the Jersey devil

The events began in January 1909, when the Jersey devil was reported in at least 30 towns. One of the earliest sightings was on Sunday 17 January at Bristol, Pennsylvania, close to the New Jersey border. At 2 a.m., John McOwen heard strange noises and got out of bed. He said: 'I looked from the window and was astonished to see a large creature standing on the banks of the canal. It looked something like an eagle . . . and it hopped along the tow-path.' Patrolman James Sackville also saw it in Bristol that night. He reported that it was winged and hopped like a bird, but had strange features and a horrible scream. Sackville ran towards it, and fired his revolver at it as it flew off. A third Bristol sighting early that same morning was made by the postmaster, E. W. Minster, who saw the Jersey devil flying over the Delaware River. The large crane-like bird seemed to be glowing, and it got close enough for Minster to see many details:

Its head resembled that of a ram, with curled horns, and its long thick neck was thrust forward in flight. It had long thin wings and short legs, the front legs shorter than the hind. Again, it uttered its mournful and awful call – a combination of a squawk and a whistle.

Bristol residents next morning found the

Jersey devil's footprints in the snow: they resembled hoofprints.

During the following week, the Jersey devil seemed to be everywhere, and its presence caused panic in the state. Farmers set steel traps and hunters followed the hoofprints. The scene must have looked like the present-day 'flaps' that occur when sightings of a bigfoot are publicised in any area, leading to an influx of photographers and hunters, with resulting chaos. But the Jersey devil seemed indifferent to the furore. On Tuesday 19 January, in the early hours, Mr and Mrs Nelson Evans of Gloucester City, New Jersey, were treated to a close-up view of the monster dancing on their shed roof for 10 minutes. Said Mr Evans later:

> It was about three feet and a half [1 metre] high, with a head like a collie dog and a face like a horse. It had a long neck, wings about two feet [60 centimetres] long, and its back legs were like those of a crane, and it had horse's hooves. It walked on its back legs and held up two short front legs with paws on them. It didn't use the front legs at all while we were watching. My wife and I were scared, I tell you, but I managed to open the window and say 'Shoo!' and it turned around, barked at me, and flew away.

Other witnesses mentioned that it had skin like an alligator's and some thought it was nearer 6 feet (1.8 metres) high.

The last sightings seem to have been on Friday 22 January, after which the Jersey devil disappeared as suddenly as it had arrived. Many facetious explanations were proposed: that it was a 'jabberwock', the 'missing link', or an 'asertoraksidimundiakins'. Mass hysteria was also put forward as an explanation.

## Common-sense explanations

Experts who took the witnesses more seriously speculated that they had seen birds: an 'invasion' of scrow-foot ducks was suggested. So, too, was a sand hill crane: with a wingspan of 80 inches (2 metres), a length of 48 inches (1.2 metres), and a 'chilling whoop for a voice', this bird was once common in New Jersey, but is now supposedly confined to remote areas of the deep South. It was also suggested that the witnesses had seen a 'prehistoric remnant'. The hoofprints were ascribed to hoaxing or to the melting and refreezing of human footprints (a possible explanation of some prints, though not those seen in inaccessible places). Which explanation you choose for the incredible events that took place between 17 and 22 January 1909 is likely to depend on your faith in the reliability of eyewitness testimony.

As we come nearer to the present day, witnesses of giant birds begin to 'identify' them as pterodactyls, a trend that may reflect increased public knowledge about prehistoric creatures. In May 1961 a businessman

In 1890 two ranchers in Arizona, USA, allegedly killed a winged monster with their Winchester rifles. The creature was colossal – over 92 feet (28 metres) long. It attacked the two men with its formidable teeth before it died. A local newspaper, the Tombstone *Epitaph*, gave a long and detailed account, but no follow-up stories appeared and no confirming evidence survives

flying a small plane over the Hudson River Valley was buzzed by a huge bird, which scarcely seemed to move its wings. He reported that it was 'a damned big bird, bigger than an eagle . . . it looked more like a pterodactyl out of the prehistoric ages.'

In the early 1960s, a couple driving at night through Trinity Forest in California saw what they thought at first was a plane in trouble, but then decided it must be a bird. It was flying at tree-top height, and seemed to have a wingspan of about 14 feet (4 metres). The couple could not discern any detail, since the 'bird' was only a silhouette to them as it flew across the road ahead, and then up a gulch towards a mine. They decided that it had looked something like a pterodactyl. Later they learned that friends of theirs had made a similar sighting in the same area and that they too had identified the 'bird' as a pterodactyl.

Early in 1976 strange reports began to emerge from Texas of sightings of creatures resembling weird birds or prehistoric flying reptiles. As usual, there were numerous 'logical' explanations for what the witnesses claimed to have seen, but the explanations rarely fitted the facts. The first sighting was made on 1 January at Harlingen by Jackie Davis (14 years old) and Tracey Lawson (11 years old). They saw a 'bird' 5 feet (1.5 metres) tall, with 'shoulders' 3 feet (90 centimetres) wide. It was black in colour with big, dark-red eyes, a bald head and a face like a gorilla's, with a sharp beak 6 inches (15 centimetres) long. Next day their parents investigated and found five tracks, which had three toes and were 8 inches (20 centimetres) across and 1½ inches (4 centimetres) deep. A man weighing 170 pounds (76.5 kilograms) was unable to make an equally deep impression in the hard ground.

A week later, on 7 January, Alvérico Guajardo saw what might have been the same bird. He had gone outside to investigate after something had hit his trailer home at Brownsville. He switched on the headlights of his station wagon and they illuminated 'something from another planet'. The creature, 4 feet (1.2 metres) long, stared at the terrified man with blazing red eyes. Guajardo saw black feathers, a beak 2 to 4 feet (60 to 80 centimetres) long, and bat-like wings. It made a horrible noise as it backed away from the lights. Guajardo finally escaped into a neighbour's house. The newspaper reporter who interviewed Guajardo the next day said he was still terrified.

Among other sightings in the state, Armando Grimaldo's experience was the most frightening. He was actually attacked by the 'bird' during the evening of 14 January as he sat in his mother-in-law's backyard at Raymondville. As he looked round to investigate a noise like the flapping of bat-like wings and a 'funny kind of whistling', he was grabbed from above by 'something with big claws'. He fled and, looking back, saw a 'bird' as big as a man, with a wingspan of between 10 and 12 feet (3 and 3.5 metres). It had a face like a bat or a monkey, big red eyes, *no* beak, and dark leathery skin, without feathers.

A big black bird with a bat-like face seen near Brownsville by Libby and Deany Ford was identified by them as a pteranodon (a

Left: the Jersey devil as portrayed by a newspaper artist in 1909. There is a whimsical air to the drawing and its headline, 'the New Jersey ''what-is-it'' ', but the sketch closely follows the verbal account of Mr and Mrs Evans, two of the many people who saw the monster. They described it as 'dancing' on their shed

Below: the sand hill crane, of imposing size and possessing a loud, penetrating cry, was invoked to explain some of the sightings of the Jersey devil that occurred in large numbers in 1909

Below: the pteranodon, related to the pterodactyl, was the largest flying creature known to science. Witnesses of mystery 'birds' often identify what they saw as a pteranodon

type of pterodactyl). On 24 February three elementary-schoolteachers driving near San Antonio also saw what they believed to be a pteranodon. As it swooped low over their cars, its shadow covered the road. They estimated its wingspan as between 15 and 20 feet (4.5 and 6 metres). Mrs Patricia Bryant said it was as big as a Piper Cub plane and that she 'could see the skeleton of this bird through the skin or feathers or whatever, and it stood out black against the background of grey feathers'. David Rendon commented that the 'bird' glided rather than flew and that it had huge bony wings like a bat's.

The most prosaic explanation for all these reports is that the witnesses were simply overawed by sightings of rare native birds. But does the pteranodon identification deserve to be taken seriously? These flying reptiles are supposed to have been extinct for 64 million years. Pterosaurs once lived in Texas and their fossils have been found there. Is it possible that any could have survived? Or – most fantastic suggestion of all – was the structure of time disrupted? Could animals living in past eras suddenly have materialised into the present day?

# Half man, half bird

**Time and again, terrifying winged humanoids have been glimpsed, on the ground or in flight, by reliable witnesses**

TALES OF HUGE BIRDS carrying off children are terrifyingly credible. The sightings of creatures resembling latter-day pterodactyls strain the powers of belief much more. But the cases we now describe would be dismissed by most people as utterly unbelievable: fantastic stories of man-like beings with wings. Yet they are told by ordinary, sincere people.

In the United States, on 18 September 1877, a winged human being was seen over Brooklyn, New York. Few details are available, but a similar figure was seen in September 1880, not far away at Coney Island. It was described in the *New York Times*, none too seriously, as 'a man with bat's wings and improved frog's legs'.

Sightings of winged humanoids seem to be more widely distributed around the globe than those of giant birds and supposed

In West Virginia, USA, a winged figure as big as a small aircraft blocked the road in front of a car in the early 1960s. It took off 'straight up' – a seemingly impossible feat for a creature of such a size. This may have been the first sighting of the Mothman, which was to be seen frequently in the state five years later

pterodactyls. The next report comes from Vladivostok, in the far eastern USSR. On 11 July 1908 a man walking in the Sikhote Alin mountains saw what looked like a man's footprint on the path ahead. His dog began to act strangely, and something could be heard trampling among the bushes. After several minutes of standing and listening, the walker, V.K. Arsenyev, threw a stone towards the unseen creature, whereupon he heard the sound of wings beating and saw something 'large and dark' fly away over the river. Unfortunately he could make out no details because of fog. Later, when Mr Arsenyev told local people what had happened, they identified the creature as 'a man who could fly in the air', well-known to hunters in the area.

A Brazilian couple, the Reals, had a closer view of 'their' winged people. Early in the 1950s they were walking one night in a wood near the sea at Pelotas in the state of Rio

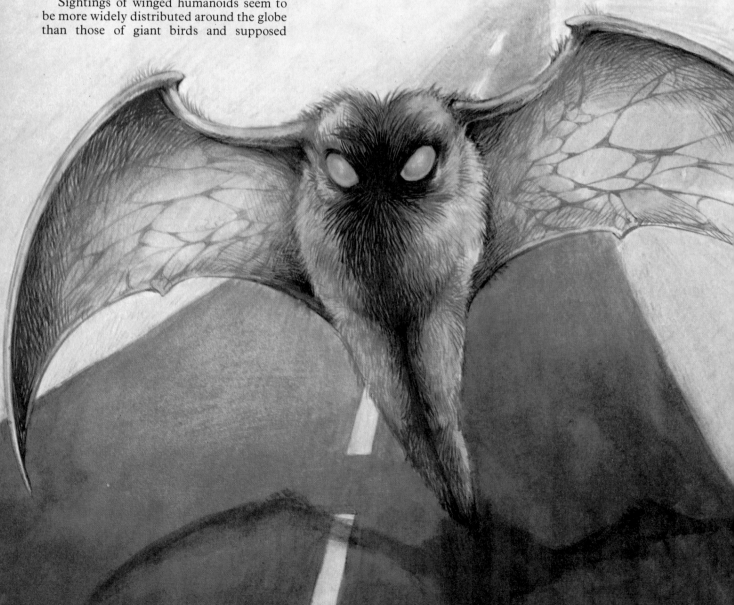

Grande do Sul when they noticed two gigantic 'birds' in the trees. As they got nearer, the 'birds' came down to the ground, and the amazed pair saw that the creatures were about 6 feet (1.8 metres) tall and looked human. They were crouching on the ground as if observing the Reals. Luiz do Rosário Real wished to approach them more closely, but his wife insisted that they return home.

A strange report describing an even closer sighting comes from Houston, Texas, USA. The night of 18 June 1953 was hot; three neighbours were sitting out on the front porch of an apartment house in the small hours. Mrs Hilda Walker said later:

We were just talking idly, when I looked up and about twenty-five feet [7·5 metres] away I saw a huge shadow across the lawn. I thought at first it was the magnified reflection of a big moth caught in a nearby street light. Then the shadow seemed to bounce upward into a pecan tree. . . . I could see him plain and could see he had big wings folded at his shoulders. There was a dim gray light all around him.

The shadow was also seen by Howard Phillips and Judy Meyers, and they described it as 'the figure of a man with wings like a bat. He was dressed in gray or black tight-fitting clothes. He stood there for about 30 seconds, swaying on the branch of the old pecan tree. Suddenly the light began to fade out slowly.' They agreed also that he was about 6½ feet (2 metres) tall and wore a black cape, tight trousers and quarter-length boots.

As the light faded, the figure seemed to melt away, and the three heard a loud swooshing noise over the houses and saw a white flash. All were adamant that they had seen this inexplicable apparition.

## First sighting of Mothman?

Not quite so clearly visible, but still definitely man-shaped, was the figure standing in the middle of the road ahead of a woman driving her father along Route 2 in the Chief Cornstalk Hunting Grounds of West Virginia, USA, in 1960 or 1961. As they got closer, the driver slowed the car. The two apprehensive witnesses saw that the grey figure was much larger than a man. The driver later reported what happened next:

A pair of wings unfolded from its back and they practically filled the whole road. It almost looked like a small airplane. Then it took off straight up . . . disappearing out of sight in seconds. We were both terrified. I stepped on the gas and raced out of there. We talked it over and decided not to tell anybody about it. Who would believe us anyway?

Who indeed? Although she did not know it, she was possibly the first witness of a winged being later nicknamed 'Mothman', which in late 1966 plagued an area of West Virginia called Point Pleasant. First to see it at that

Above: Mothman was said to lack any visible arms or head, to have luminous red eyes and huge wings, and to be bigger than a man

Below: a 'birdwoman' flew so close to three marines in Vietnam that they could hear her wings flapping

time were two young local couples, Mr and Mrs Roger Scarberry and Mr and Mrs Steve Mallette. Late on the night of 15 November they were driving through the 'TNT area' where there was an abandoned wartime explosives factory. As they passed an old generator plant, they saw in the darkness two bright red circles, which looked like eyes. As the circles moved, the couples saw a man-shaped figure, between 6 and 7 feet (1·8 and 2 metres) tall, greyish in colour and with big folded wings; it was shuffling along on two legs.

Roger, who was driving, quickly turned the car in the direction of safety and they drove off at speed. But they saw the creature, or another similar one, standing near the road and as they went past it spread its bat-like wings and began to follow them. Even though they accelerated to 100 miles per hour (160 km/h), the 'bird' kept pace with them – without flapping its wings. Mrs Mallette could hear it squeaking 'like a big mouse'. When they reported their experience at the sheriff's office, the deputy could see they were scared and he drove straight to the TNT area, but saw nothing strange.

The story was publicised and Point Pleasant immediately became a focus of attention for monster-hunters. Armed men searched the TNT area but did not find their prey. However, Mothman was still around: on the evening of 16 November he appeared to Mrs

Mawnan "Bird-Man" based on sketch by June Melling, witnessed and drawn 17/4/76.

Birdman monster. Seen on 3rd July, quite late at night but not quite dark. Red eyes. Black mouth. It was very big with great big wings and black claws. Feathers grey. B. Perry 4th July 1976.

I saw this monster 'bird last night .It stood like a man then it flew up though the trees. It is as big as a man .Its eyes are red and shine brightly. Sally Chapman 4/7/76.

brown in colour and man-shaped but without any arms or head. It had luminous bright red eyes where a man's shoulders would be. The wings were folded back when not in use, and the wingspread was about 10 feet (3 metres). The majority of sightings were made in November and December 1966; then Mothman was gone.

Three marines on guard duty near Da Nang in South Vietnam, in July or August 1969, got a closer view of the extraordinary entity that flew over them in the early hours of the morning. The story was later told by one of them, Earl Morrison:

All of a sudden – I don't know why – we all three looked out there in the sky and we saw this figure coming toward us. It had a kind of glow and we couldn't make out what it was at first. It started coming toward us, real slowly. All of a sudden we saw what looked like wings, like a bat's, only it was gigantic compared to what a regular bat would be. After it got close enough so we could see what it was, it looked like a woman. A naked woman. She was black. Her skin was black, her body was black, the wings were black, everything was black. But it glowed. It glowed in the night – kind of a greenish cast to it.

The three saw her long enough to notice that she had arms, hands and fingers, but that these were joined to her wings. They just stood and watched as she flew overhead, a couple of yards above them.

### The Cornish Owlman

Sometimes, as in this report, the sightings have been single ones, the mysterious winged entity afterwards disappearing as if it never existed. And sometimes, as in West Virginia in 1966, there have been repeated sightings in a small area, but still without any real clues emerging as to the nature of the apparition. Perhaps the strangest series of reports of 'winged things' are those concerning the 'Owlman', seen in Cornwall, England, in 1976 and again in 1978. The Owlman's territory was very small – the area around Mawnan Church on the south coast.

He was first seen on 17 April 1976, hovering over the church tower, by June Melling (12 years old) and her sister Vicky (9 years old). June described and drew a feathered birdman. Nearly three months passed before the second sighting, made on 3 July. Again the witnesses were young girls: 14-year-old Sally Chapman and Barbara Perry. They were camping in the woods and at about 10 p.m. they realised that they were not alone. They heard a strange hissing noise, and then saw a figure standing not far away among the pine trees. Sally described what they saw:

It was like a big owl with pointed ears, as big as a man. The eyes were red and glowing. At first, I thought it was someone dressed up, playing a joke,

Marcella Bennett who was visiting friends living in the TNT area. She was sitting in the parked car when she noticed a figure in the darkness. 'It seemed as if it had been lying down. It rose up slowly from the ground. A big gray thing. Bigger than a man, with terrible glowing red eyes.' Like the two couples on the previous night, Mrs Bennett seemed hypnotised by Mothman's red eyes. As she stood there staring at it, she and her baby daughter were grabbed by a friend and dragged into the house.

During the following days, numerous people saw Mothman – or believed they did. How many of the sightings were caused by the 'contagion' of news stories, we shall never know. The writer John Keel went to the Point Pleasant area to investigate at first hand. From the many reports he collected, he established that Mothman was between 5 and 7 feet (1·5 and 2 metres) tall, grey or

Drawings made by three young witnesses of the Cornish Owlman, with their own descriptions. The resemblance between the sighting of 3 July and the one made three months earlier is striking

trying to scare us. I laughed at it, we both did, then it went up in the air and we both screamed. When it went up, you could see its feet were like pincers. Barbara added: 'It's true. It was horrible, a nasty owl-face with big ears and big red eyes. It was covered in grey feathers. The claws on its feet were black. It just flew straight up and disappeared in the treetops.'

The next day, 4 July, yet another young girl, Jane Greenwood, along with her sister, saw the Owlman. Jane described what they saw in a letter to the local paper:

It was Sunday morning and the place was in the trees near Mawnan Church, above the rocky beach. It was in the trees standing like a full-grown man, but the legs bent backwards like a bird's. It saw us and quickly jumped up and rose straight up through the trees.

My sister and I saw it very clearly

before it rose up. It has red slanting eyes and a very large mouth. The feathers are silvery grey and so are his body and legs. The feet are like big, black crab's claws.

We were frightened at the time. It was so strange, like something in a horror film. After the thing went up there was crackling sounds in the tree tops for ages.

Later that day we spoke to some people at the camp-site, who said they had seen the Morgawr Monster on Saturday, when they were swimming with face masks and snorkels in the river, below where we saw the bird man. They saw it underwater, and said it was enormous and shaped like a lizard.

Our mother thinks we made it all up just because we read about these

The Owlman sightings took place in an area of ancient significance: near Mawnan Church, which was built inside a prehistoric earthwork (below). Sally Chapman and Barbara Perry encountered the creature in nearby woods (bottom)

things, but that is not true. We really saw the bird man, though it could have been somebody playing a trick in very good costume and make-up.

But how could it rise up like that? If we imagined it, then we both imagined the same thing at the same time.

The 'Morgawr Monster' she refers to is a sea monster that was also putting in regular appearances in Falmouth Bay during 1976. UFOs were seen in the area too – Falmouth Bay was the best place to be in 1976 if you longed for a strange experience.

After July 1976 the Owlman apparently did not reappear until June 1978. Early that month a 16-year-old girl saw 'a monster, like a devil, flying up through the trees near old Mawnan Church.' On 2 August three young French girls also saw him near the church. They were frightened by something 'very big, like a great big furry bird'. It was white with a 'gaping mouth and big round eyes'.

Why should strange events occur together at certain points on the globe? If some form of energy, known or unknown, is involved in the genesis of these strange happenings, it would seem that it tends to focus or concentrate in limited areas at specific times. The result is an upsurge in sightings of monsters and UFOs, and an increase in strange happenings of all kinds.

Doubtless there will be waves of sightings of weird winged creatures again. But, as with UFOs and the bigfoot, it seems very unlikely that we shall acquire unambiguous physical traces of the things seen – we cannot count on having a corpse to study. The phenomena seem too elusive.

# Monsters of the deep

**For thousands of years, sightings of strange sea monsters have been reported around the world. Here, JANET and COLIN BORD argue that the ocean depths contain many creatures as yet unknown to science, and that these reports should not be discounted as wild imaginings**

Below: a drawing of a 'most dreadful monster' seen off the coast of Greenland by Norwegian missionary Hans Egede in 1734. Known as the Apostle of Greenland, Hans Egede was a pious and honest man who took a keen interest in natural history

WITH MORE THAN 60 per cent of the Earth's surface covered with water, it is hardly surprising that sightings of giant underwater monsters have been reported since antiquity. Even today, marine biologists, who have long been aware of the vast unexplored depths of the Earth's oceans, cautiously accept that the numerous reports of sea monster sightings seem to provide evidence that many creatures, at present unknown and unclassified, may be living in the dark and hidden waters.

The Biblical beast of evil, the leviathan ('the twisting serpent . . . the dragon that is in the sea') is mentioned in the Old Testament five times, and from the Norsemen to the Aborigines in Australia, from the Chinese to the American Indians, ancient mythologies speak of giant sea serpents.

Many of the early reports of sea monsters were collected by Scandinavian ecclesiastics. Archbishop Olaf Mansson, now better known as Olaus Magnus, who was exiled to Rome after the Swedish Reformation in the early 16th century, published a natural history of the northern lands in 1555 that contained reports of sea serpents. He described a sea serpent 200 feet (60 metres) long and 20 feet (6 metres) thick that would eat calves, lambs and hogs, and would even pluck men from boats. Archbishop Magnus also stated that the monster's appearance foretold disasters such as wars.

Interestingly, Magnus described the sea serpent as being black, having hair hanging from its neck (or mane), shining eyes, and putting its 'head on high like a pillar'. These characteristics also appear in recent sighting reports, suggesting that Olaus Magnus was writing about originally factual reports that had become distorted and embroidered with much retelling.

Two hundred years later historians were still recording sightings of sea serpents, though the clergy still maintained that these were sightings of the beast of evil. On 6 July 1734 a sea monster appeared off the coast of Greenland, and was reported by a Norwegian missionary, Hans Egede. In 1741 he wrote that its body was as bulky as a ship and was three or four times as long, and that it leapt from the water and plunged back again.

Another 18th-century writer on the mystery of the sea serpent was the Bishop of Bergen, Erik Pontoppidan. After detailed enquiry he found that hardly a year went by without some sea serpent sightings along the Scandinavian coastline and he published his findings in 1752.

A year earlier Bishop Pontoppidan had arranged for a letter from Captain Lorenz von Ferry to be read to the Bergen Court of Justice, in which was described a sea serpent that the Captain and his crew had seen in 1746 while rowing ashore to Molde in Norway. He said it had a grey head like a

Above: the eminent British naturalist, Sir Joseph Banks (1743–1820). In 1820 he affirmed his 'full faith in the existence of our Serpent in the Sea'

Right: when the crew of a French ship were saved from death at the hands of a frightful monster, they gave a painting of the event, in thanksgiving for their deliverance, to a church in St Malo. The original disappeared, but the French naturalist, Denys de Montfort, had a copy made in the 1790s (shown here), as he felt it confirmed the existence of giant sea monsters

horse, large black eyes, a black mouth and a long white mane. Behind the head seven or eight coils could be seen above the water. Captain von Ferry fired at it and it sank below the water and did not reappear. Two of his seamen, who had also been witnesses, swore on oath that the contents of the report were true.

During the 18th century, the increasing importance attached to rational scientific analysis resulted in mariners' reports of monstrous sea beasts being discounted, then openly derided. A Norwegian scientist, Peter Ascanius, stated that sailors who saw a line of humps in the water were not viewing a huge water beast, but were in fact seeing a line of leaping dolphins. This doubtful explanation has since become a favourite standby for debunkers of sea monster reports.

However, perhaps surprisingly, naturalists who took the time to study the reports almost invariably pronounced in favour of the sea serpent's existence. These included Sir Joseph Banks, a leading British scientist in the early 19th century who sailed round the world with Captain Cook, and Thomas

Huxley, who in 1893 wrote that there was no reason why snake-like reptiles 50 feet (15 metres) or more in length should not be found in the sea.

American marine biologists of repute at this time agreed that the sea could very well contain unknown species of monstrous creatures and a curator of the London Zoological Gardens, A. D. Bartlett, wrote in 1877 that it was unwise to disregard the evidence from so many different sources.

Constantin Samuel Rafinesque was a brilliant and controversial naturalist, who made a tremendous contribution to the

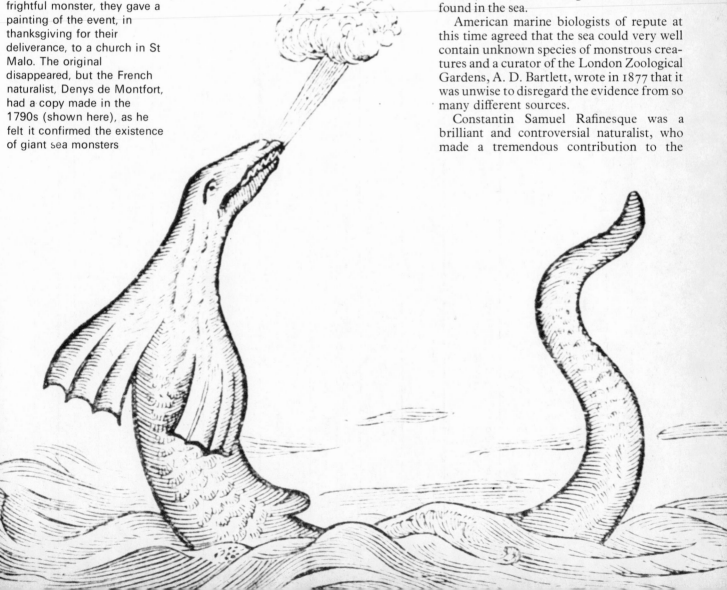

sea monster in nature. His book, *The great sea serpent*, published in 1892, is based on 187 sighting reports and was a courageous work in the contemporary sceptical climate, but it is marred by his preconception that there is only one kind of unknown sea monster, closely related to the seal family.

As one would expect, sea monsters have long been a part of mariners' tales. Some reports have undoubtedly been exaggerated, but many others that made their way into ships' logs are strangely consistent.

In May 1901, when the officers on the bridge of the steamer *Grangense* in the western Atlantic saw a monstrous crocodile-like creature with 6-inch (15-centimetre) long teeth, splashing about on the surface, the Captain refused to note the encounter in the ship's log, saying: 'They will say we were all drunk, and I'll thank you, Mister, not to mention it to our agents at Para or Manaus.'

But there were others who were perhaps less careful of their reputation, such as

Left: Thomas Huxley (1825–1895) was another noted British scientist who pronounced in favour of giant sea serpents

Below: on 6 August 1848, Captain M'Quhae and six members of the crew of HMS *Daedalus* sighted a 60-foot (18-metre) serpent in the southern–Atlantic. When an illustrated report of the encounter appeared in the British press, it caused a fierce controversy

Bottom: one of the sea monsters described by Archbishop Olaus Magnus and illustrated in his history of Scandinavia, which was published in 1555

knowledge of American flora and fauna. Born in 1783, he emigrated to America from Europe in 1815 where he became Professor of Natural Sciences at Transylvania University, in Kentucky. Among his wide range of interests was the sea serpent, of whose existence he was fully convinced.

During the first half of the 19th century there were a great many sightings of sea serpents along the north-east American coast, centred on the fishing port of Gloucester, in Massachusetts. Rafinesque examined the reports and decided that they fell into four groups, to which he gave the generic name of *Megophias*, or 'big snake'.

However, there were many opponents of scientists who were investigating the unexplained phenomenon of sea monsters. Among the more vociferous was Sir Richard Owen, an influential but conservative scientist of the 19th century, whom Darwin called 'one of my chief enemies'.

In 1848 Owen conducted a correspondence of some acerbity with Captain Peter M'Quhae, through the columns of *The Times*. Their debate concerned the 60-foot (18-metre) sea serpent that the Captain and his crew had seen in the southern Atlantic from the deck of HMS *Daedalus* on 6 August that year. Although Owen used the sceptic's customary ploy of interpreting the report to fit his own preconceptions (in this case his identification was a sealion), Captain M'Quhae would have none of it and firmly maintained that he had seen a sea serpent.

Antoon Cornelis Oudemans was a Dutch biologist who came from a family of scientists. Born in 1858, he studied biology at Utrecht and became an authority on mites and ticks. He also brought his scientific skills to bear on the problem of the sea monster.

Throughout his long life (he died in 1943) Oudemans collected many sighting reports and continued to speculate on the place of the

Despite scathing criticism from 19th-century scientists, sightings of sea monsters continued to be reported. The painting above shows a monster sinking a ship off the coast of Massachusetts in 1819, an area where giant sea creatures seemed to thrive

Lieutenant George Sandford who, as captain of the merchant ship *Lady Combermere*, in 1820 reported seeing in mid-Atlantic a serpent 60 to 100 feet (18 to 30 metres) long, spouting water like a whale. On 15 May 1833 four British Army officers and a military store-keeper were out for a day's fishing when they saw an 80-foot (24-metre) long serpent swim by, not more than 200 yards (180 metres) away. This was at Mahone Bay, 40 miles (65 kilometres) west of Halifax, Nova Scotia, and so convinced were they of the importance of their sighting that they all signed a statement and added:

There could be no mistake, no delusion, and we were all perfectly satisfied that we had been favoured with a view of the 'true and veritable sea-serpent', which had been generally considered to have existed only in the brain of some Yankee skipper, and treated as a tale not much entitled to belief.

Another sighting of the crocodile-like type of sea monster was made by the captain and crew of the *Eagle* on 23 March 1830, a few hours before they docked at Charleston, South Carolina. Captain Deland sailed his schooner to within 25 yards (22 metres) of the basking creature and fired a musket at its head. When the bullet hit, the monster dived beneath the ship and struck it several times with its tail, blows strong enough to damage the craft if not to sink her.

Another military man who had a close-up view of an unknown monster from the depths was Major H. W. J. Senior of the Bengal Staff Corps. He was travelling on the *City of Baltimore* in the Gulf of Aden on 28 January 1879 and saw 500 yards (450 metres) from the ship a head with a 2-foot (60-centimetre) diameter neck protrude from the water to a height of 20 or 30 feet (6 or 9 metres). The creature was moving so rapidly he was unable to focus his field glasses upon it as it rose up, opened its mouth wide and closed it again before submerging, only to reappear a few moments later. No body was visible, but Major Senior described the head as of a bulldog-like appearance. His report was also signed by other witnesses.

In the 100 years since this sighting, sea monsters have continued to surface before startled onlookers. The intrepid trans–Atlantic rower Captain John Ridgway saw a monster just before midnight on 25 July 1966. His companion, Sergeant Chay Blyth, who has since became a world-famous yachtsman, was asleep. As Ridgway rowed he heard a swishing noise and a 35-foot (10-metre) long sea serpent outlined in phosphorescence, 'as if a string of neon lights were hanging from it', came swimming towards the boat. It dived underneath and did not reappear on the other side.

## An ocean giant

Many zoologists believe the kraken – the legendary Norwegian sea monster – probably refers to the giant squids of the genus *Architeuthis*. These creatures inhabit the depths of the ocean and can grow to lengths of over 60 feet (18 metres). The sperm whale is the only animal brave enough to tackle these monsters and fierce battles take place between them.

The giant squid shown here was stranded at Ranheim, Norway, in 1954. Though not the largest specimen known to science, its overall length was 30 feet (9 metres).

# From the sea serpent to the super-otter

**Besides classic sightings of sea monsters there are 'classic' hoaxes, too. But this does not mean that we should discount the existence of unknown creatures. And, as JANET and COLIN BORD show, using the techniques pioneered by the Belgian zoologist Bernard Heuvelmans the whole subject can now be studied scientifically**

MANY SCIENTISTS remain sceptical about the existence of underwater monsters, yet sightings of giant sea creatures, some extremely detailed, continue to be reported around the world.

An active monster of recent years, sighted off the coast of Cornwall, England, is known as Morgawr (Cornish for 'sea giant'). This was seen quite often during 1975 and 1976, in Falmouth Bay, and on 5 March 1976 two photographs of it were published in the *Falmouth Packet*. Although these were submitted anonymously, nevertheless they do appear very convincing, showing a long-necked creature similar to that reported to be in Loch Ness.

Another strange creature has been seen in the waters of Cardigan Bay off the west coast of Wales. On 2 March 1975, six local schoolgirls were walking along the beach at dusk when 200 yards (180 metres) away a creature moved across the beach towards the sea. They described it as being 10 feet (3 metres) long with a long neck and tail and large green eyes. They were quite terrified at this spectacle and ran away to report it to the coastguard. Later they described it to their art teacher, Colin Palmer, who drew the creature. When he showed his sketch to the crew of a fishing boat, who had seen a monster when they were fishing off Bardsey Sound,

The Cornish sea monster Morgawr was sighted several times during 1975 and 1976. 'Mary F' succeeded in photographing the creature, of which 15 to 18 feet (5 to 6 metres) were visible, in February 1976 at Rosemullion Head, near Falmouth

there was 'instant recognition'.

The consequences of the publicity attached to famous sightings are twofold: there is a sudden increase in similar reports, many of which turn out to be well-authenticated, and a subsequent crop of hoaxes. Researchers are, of course, keen to expose the latter. Spurious reports are intended to bring ridicule on those who believe them, so eventually they must be revealed to make their point.

A hoax report that contained, perhaps deliberately, a clue to its true nature was published by the *Globe* in 1848, scarcely a week after *The Times* had published an account of a sea serpent seen by Peter M'Quhae, Captain of HMS *Daedalus*.

The hoax was printed in the form of a

subsequent enquiries revealed that the letter was a hoax.

Over 100 years later, in March 1965, an Australian magazine published an article on 'the Great Barrier Reef monster' by a Frenchman, Robert Le Serrec. He reported that he and his family had been camping on an island on the Great Barrier Reef where they had found a sea serpent, over 80 feet (24 metres) long and lying injured in the shallow lagoon water.

After cautiously circling around the creature in their boat and taking photographs, Le Serrec and his companion, Henk de Jong, entered the water armed with a rifle and a camera. As the two men approached to within 20 feet (6 metres) and took pictures, the creature turned its massive head towards them and opened its mouth threateningly. They quickly returned to their boat and the monster swam out to sea.

The story and photographs were also offered to an American magazine, whose

Above: until the Age of Enlightenment in the 18th century, people still thought of the oceans as full of fearsome monsters. In this 16th-century engraving, the whale is depicted as a huge creature with terrible fangs and claws

Right and below right: this strange-looking carcase with its huge head and duck-like beak was washed up on the rocks at Santa Cruz, California, in 1925. Decomposition made the specimen hard to identify but, after examining the skull, the Museum of the California Academy of Sciences showed that the carcase was that of an extremely rare beaked whale

letter, posted on 19 October in Glasgow and purporting to be from James Henderson, captain of the Mary Ann. He wrote that on 20 September Captain Mark Trelawny of the brig *Daphne* had seen 'a huge serpent, or snake, with a dragon's head', and the captain had loaded a gun with scrap-iron and fired at it. The 100-foot (30-metre) long monster had foamed and lashed the water and made off at 16 knots.

*The Times* reprinted the story and a keen-eyed correspondent wrote to ask how the *Daphne* had manged to travel from the encounter to Lisbon, where Captain Trelawny had told Captain Henderson of his experience, in only 10 days. The distance covered was 5000 miles (8000 kilometres) and would have called for an average speed of 20 knots. The correspondent drily remarked: 'Probably the serpent took the brig in tow' –

An ancient Greek vase showing Heracles struggling with the river god Achelous to win Deianira. The god is represented with the torso of a man and the body of a sea serpent

editor asked Ivan T. Sanderson, the British biologist and investigator of the unexplained, his opinion of them. Le Serrec's background in France was also investigated. Here it was found that he had tried to finance his expedition by telling prospective financial backers that he would make a lot of money on the trip in a venture connected with a giant sea serpent.

Biologists who examined the photographs and descriptions were not satisfied that they portrayed a genuine animal. Its eyes were too far back on the top of its head and Le Serrec's story was not entirely consistent.

The various investigations all pointed to a hoax, probably achieved by filling a long plastic tube with air and sinking it with stones. Needless to say, the American magazine did not publish the story.

The sceptical scientist asks for physical

remains to examine, and periodically, strange, large carcases are washed up on remote beaches. Owing to pressure of other work and the remoteness of the locations, these are usually ignored or identified at a distance as the remains of a known sea creature, often a basking shark.

The 55-foot (17-metre) long body that was washed up on the shore of the island of Stronsay in the Orkneys in 1808, was first seen by local fishermen and farmers but, before any informed examination could be made, storms had smashed the rotting carcase to pieces. The drawing that was made from the witnesses' descriptions showed an extraordinary animal with a long neck and undulating tail and three pairs of legs, a feature hitherto unknown in a vertebrate.

The corpse was finally identified as a shark by a British surgeon, Everard Home, who had made a study of shark anatomy and was able to obtain specimens of bones that had been removed from the beast. When shark carcases are washed up on shore, the rapid decomposition of certain parts of the anatomy, namely the lower jaw, the lower tail fluke and the fins, leaves what looks like a weird creature with a long thin neck and tail.

In 1925 an unidentified carcase was cast ashore at Santa Cruz, California. It appeared to have a 30-foot (9-metre) long neck and a huge beaked head, but was eventually identified as the remains of a very rare beaked whale from the North Pacific.

The large decomposing 'glob' that was washed up on a remote beach in western Tasmania in July 1960 received little official attention until March 1962. Then scientists from Hobart located the exact spot from the air and a group went to investigate. Helicopters were used to carry away samples, and the official statement said that the object was 'a large lump of decomposing blubber, probably torn off a whale'. However, the other

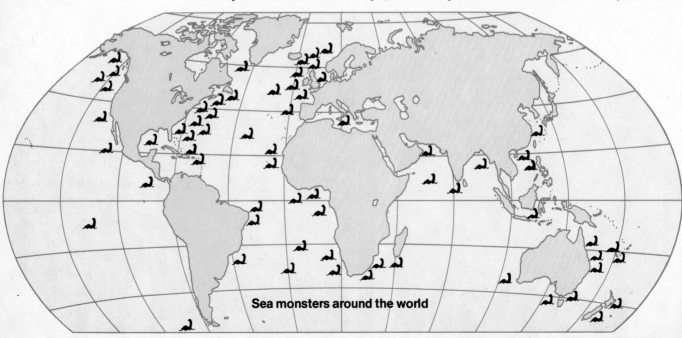

**Sea monsters around the world**

biologists who had been following the case thought that this was unlikely.

A more recent find occurred on 25 April 1977, when the Japanese trawler *Zuiyo Maru* hauled up a large, partially rotted carcase 28 miles (45 kilometres) east of Christchurch, New Zealand. Concerned that it might contaminate his catch, the captain, Akira Tanaka, had it photographed and drawn, then dropped it back in the sea. The incident intrigued the world's press and a television film crew flew from Japan to cover the story. Although the ship's crew were convinced that they had seen an unknown monster, the

Right: the long-necked sea serpent appears to be the most common of the nine specific types of sea monster classified by Belgian zoologist Dr Bernard Heuvelmans. Analysis of 48 certain sightings indicate that the creature is between 15 and 65 feet (5 and 20 metres) long and moves through the water with exceptional speed for an animal of this size

Long-necked

photographs suggest a decomposed shark.

Some of the most convincing evidence for the existence of sea monsters comes from those areas where they have been sighted repeatedly over decades or even centuries. In the Strait of Georgia between Vancouver Island and British Columbia, off the west coast of Canada, the creature known locally as Cadborosaurus or Caddy was sighted by the Indians long before the arrival of the white settlers.

In this century an early sighting of Caddy was made by F. W. Kemp, a local government official. On 10 August 1932, Mr Kemp was with his wife and son when they saw it swim at terrific speed through the water. Caddy was seen frequently during the 1930s and in 1950 was sighted by Judge James Brown and his family, when it appeared as a 45-foot (14-metre) long serpent that rose out of the water several times. Mrs. R. A. Stewart, who saw it in 1963 when fishing with her husband, was terrified by its wide-open jaws.

Further south on the American west coast is San Clemente Island, a favourite area for deep-sea angling and an area where water

Above and right: a recent find that attracted world-wide attention was the carcase hauled on board the Japanese trawler *Zuiyo Maru* in 1977. Concerned that the carcase might contaminate his catch, Captain Akira Tanaka had it photographed, then threw it back in the sea. Biologists believe that the photographs show a decomposed shark and not an unknown monster

monsters have been seen frequently throughout this century. When technical fishing writer J. Charles Davis interviewed numerous independent witnesses, he found their descriptions tallied to an amazing degree. Many of the witnesses were wealthy members of the big-game fishing clubs, who knew what to expect from the sea and had no desire to lay themselves open to ridicule.

Why does the sea serpent still remain comparatively unknown? One reason might be that although more than 60 per cent of the Earth's surface is covered by water, very little of it is travelled over by commercial

### Many-humped

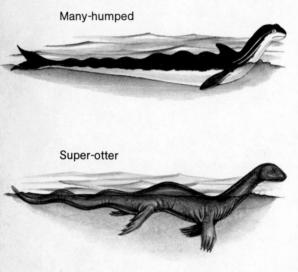

### Super-otter

Left: the many-humped sea serpent and the super-otter are about the same size – 60-100 feet (18-20 metres) long. The many-humped category has been seen chiefly along the coast of New England, USA, though the number of sightings has diminished since the beginning of this century. As there has been no sighting of the super-otter since 1848, Dr Heuvelmans believes it may now be extinct

Right: the main characteristic of the many-finned sea serpent is breath blown out of the nostrils. It grows to a length of more than 60 feet (18 metres) and has been sighted only in tropical waters. The last mammal in Heuvelmans' classification is the merhorse, which has huge eyes and a reddish mane. It has been sighted in most waters of the world, apart from the Indian Ocean and the Polar seas

shipping, which follows fixed and narrow routes. The vibrations made by engines and bow waves are sufficient to keep timid sea creatures away from these areas, in contrast to the days of sail when the silent ships relied on wind and currents and were often driven well off their routes.

The cases cited above, and the hundreds of others that can be found in the various works on the subject, point to the fact that there is not just one type of sea monster. In 1965, Belgian zoologist Dr Bernard Heuvelmans completed the most detailed and exhaustive work on the subject in recent times – *In the wake of the sea-serpents*, a book that has been of great value to all modern writers on water monsters. In it, Dr Heuvelmans describes and analyses more than 500 reports, dating from 1639 to 1964. From these reports he draws certain conclusions and here we attempt a brief summary of them.

Of the 587 sightings that Heuvelmans collected, 56 of them he considered most likely to be hoaxes. Another group were known sea creatures mistakenly reported as unknown monsters – he found 52 of these. Another 121 reports were removed from his final analysis because the details given were too vague or ambiguous for any useful classification to be made.

This left 358 sightings with various characteristics of appearance and behaviour that could be divided into nine types. These

range from the most frequently seen 'long-necked' sea serpent, which has a cigar-shaped body, four webbed feet and is a fast swimmer, to the very infrequently seen marine saurians that look like crocodiles 50–60 feet (15–18 metres) long and have only been seen in mid-ocean tropical waters.

The other types Dr Heuvelmans names informally as merhorses, many-humped, super-otters, many-finned, super-eels, fathers-of-all-the-turtles and yellow-bellies. He has also found a group he calls 'ambiguous periscopes', which might be either long-necked monsters or super-eels. He

### Many-finned

### Merhorse

considers the long-necked serpent and the first four categories above to be mammals.

The super-eel is probably a fish whose normal habitat is the ocean depths and when seen on the surface is usually near death, while the marine saurian could well be a survivor from the Jurassic period that normally lives well below the surface and so has survived to the present. His yellow-belly group is somewhat more difficult to classify owing to a lack of detailed descriptions, but it could possibly be a fish, perhaps a shark.

Another interesting observation that Dr Heuvelmans has made is that the most frequent sightings during this century have been of the long-necked sea monster, which as a species may be on the increase. Conversely, there has been no sighting of the super-otter since 1848 and Heuvelmans suggests that these two are, or have been, in competition for the same ecological niche – the super-otter must be the loser and it may well now be extinct.

The world beneath the sea has still not been fully explored and, despite the sceptics, there appears to be abundant evidence for the existence of large, unknown sea creatures. Scientists believe that before long they will have a much more detailed knowledge of life in the ocean depths – indeed, new species are being discovered every year, so perhaps they will soon find the answer to the mystery of the underwater monster.

## American Lake Monsters

**Thousands of lakes are scattered across North America – and from many come tales of huge creatures, rivalling the legends of the Loch Ness monster and the sea serpents. PETER COSTELLO tells some of the stories of Nessie's North American cousins**

THE LAKES OF NORTH AMERICA, both in the United States and in Canada, have produced more reports of monsters than any other continent. More than 90 lakes and rivers are credited with being haunts of 'unidentified swimming objects'. Few of these reports are backed up with anything as concrete as photographs or ciné film. Most of them remain unexplained, some of the most intriguing of modern zoological mysteries. If there are so many creatures at large in these lakes, what are they and how do they manage to remain so elusive?

Reports of American lake monsters have a very long history. Naturally enough, the original inhabitants of the continent, the Indians, had many legends of large water monsters. As with all folklore, their graphic details may well conceal something very real.

The Mic-Mac Indians of the Nova Scotia area believed in a 'fabulous snake', which was similar to one described by the Algonquin further west. The Iroquois of upper New York state had a monster called Onijore. In Indiana, the Potawatomi believed in a monster in Lake Manitou on the Wabash River; in the early 19th century they objected to the erection of a mill that would have disturbed the creature's way of life.

Lake Ontario, straddling the Canada/United States border, lies under a sheet of winter ice. Occasional sightings of monsters have been made here and in other Great Lakes. But the most frequently reported lake creature is Ogopogo, a denizen of Lake Okanagan in British Columbia.
The model of Ogopogo (inset) is part of the lake shore dwellers' publicity

# Lake monsters of the New World

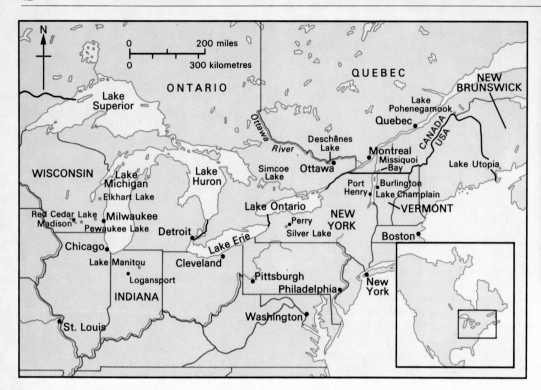

Above: the Lake Utopia monster pursues a canoe in this contemporary drawing from an issue of the *Canadian Illustrated News* of 1872. According to the highly coloured account of the witnesses, the monster had 'bloody jaws'

Left: north-eastern North America, a region once covered by glaciers, which gouged thousands of lakes out of the land. Have prehistoric aquatic animals escaped extinction in these sheltered waters?

Below: Lake Champlain, the reputed home of the Champ, who, whether he exists or not, enjoys legal protection from hunters

These Indian tribes were grouped around the area of the Great Lakes. Further west, in the Rocky Mountain states, there were other legends. Among the Shawnee there was a legend of a great reptile, which was killed by a magician with the aid of a young girl – like the legend of St George and the Dragon. The Kalapuya Indians of the Willamette River in Oregon believed in a monster called Aturki, which lived in the lakes, rivers and pools of that region. An anthropologist remarked that 'those who saw it described it as resembling a seal or a sea otter.' Were these mere myths? Or descriptions of extraordinary but real animals?

The earliest reports, as distinct from legends, come from the first decades of the 19th century. It is often said that the first report of an American lake monster was made by the great French explorer of Canada, Samuel de Champlain, in 1609, when he discovered the great lake in Vermont now named after him. But this is not so: this is one 'report' that can safely be ascribed to an error on the part of a journalist. The story has been taken up by every writer on Lake Champlain since the error was made in 1960. Champlain does indeed mention a frightful water monster, but that was supposed to haunt the sea coast of the St Lawrence estuary, which is far to the north-east.

One of the pioneers of sea serpent research, naturalist Constantin Samuel Rafinesque, noted that there was a tradition of 'a great Water Snake', which lived in a lake near Philadelphia. But he also collected reports of newer sightings:

On the 3rd of July, 1817, one was seen in Lake Erie, three miles [5 kilometres] from land, by the crew of a schooner, which was 35 or 40 feet [10.5 or 12

metres] long, and one foot [30 centimetres] in diameter; its colour was dark mahogany, nearly black. This account is very imperfect, and does not even notice if it had scales; therefore it must remain doubtful whether it was a snake or a fish. I am inclined to believe it was a fish.

In 1819 the animal was seen again, 'and described to be of a copper colour, with bright eyes, and 60 feet [18 metres] long'. Shooting at it seemed to have no effect: whether because it was protected by scales or because the marksmanship was poor.

At this time the New England sea serpent was taken very seriously. A report of a monster in Lake Ontario (with which Lake Erie connects) was even dignified by publication in a German scientific journal in 1835.

## Monsters in limbo

Soon lake monsters joined sea serpents in that limbo to which 'respectable' journals consign them nowadays. No one was to take them so seriously again for a long time. They became a suitable topic for humorous journalism and for hoaxes.

During 1855 Silver Lake in New York state was the scene of a great sensation: a 'sea serpent' had been sighted in the lake. There were numerous reports of sightings and the local press took up the tale. Over the next couple of years the sightings faded away. Then there was a fire at the local hotel, and in the attic volunteer firemen discovered the remains of the 'sea serpent'. It was a dummy, kept afloat with compressed air, which the hotel owner had made to boost his business. Local people were angry at first; later the perpetrator of the hoax was forgiven. Today the town of Perry holds a periodic sea serpent

Below: the skyline of Buffalo, New York state, rises above the waters of Lake Erie. Sightings of monsters in the lake date from the early 19th century – but they occurred before the severe pollution of the lake

Bottom: Naitaka, the monster spirit of Lake Okanagan, depicted in a rock carving made by the Shushwap Indians. When Indians travelled on the lake, they would drop a chicken or pup into the waters as an offering to Naitaka: failure to do so would incur his wrath

festival to commemorate the hoax.

Journalists in America were often responsible for creating instant folklore. In the 1830s, for instance, there came a series of reports from the lakes of Indiana in the Middle West. There had been, of course, earlier Indian legends. But then came reports, published in the Logansport newspaper, that white settlers had also been seeing monsters. These reports were investigated a century later by a professor of history at Indiana University. Donald Smalley discovered that they may well have been a journalistic 'joke'. As the last Indians were moved out of the state, the reports faded away.

In Canada, too, in areas then on the frontier, there were many reports. The most striking of these came from Lake Utopia, in New Brunswick, in 1867. Lumbermen employed at a mill on the lake were surprised to see some object splashing about in the water. The report that it was a large animal caused great excitement. In 1872 the monster was written up in the *Canadian Illustrated News* with an astonishing woodcut of the creature curling through the water in pursuit of two men in a canoe. It had a head as large as a barrel, 'snapping its bloody jaws in a most horrible manner'. The monster was said to appear soon after the winter ice had broken up, which brought many visitors to the lake in March each year in the hope of seeing it.

One witness in the early 1950s was a Mrs Fred McKillop. Alone one day, she saw a large black shape churning up the water, and moving backwards and forwards at great speed.

For some scientists, anxious to explain away reports of lake monsters, this churning of the water holds a clue to what some 'monsters' might be. In Norway it was found that many reports came from mountain lakes

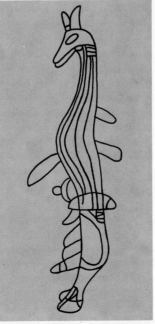

on the shores of which there were saw mills. On one famous occasion one of these 'monsters' was investigated by a policeman after it had surfaced in a patch of churning water. It turned out to be a great mass of sawdust and other vegetable rubbish, lifted to the surface of the water by the expanding gases created by its own rotting.

Were the Lake Utopia monster sightings caused by masses of decaying vegetation? But if so, what was it that chased the Indians? What of the reports from other lakes? What of the descriptions of long-necked creatures? Theories of this kind have to be seen in a wider context of reports from all over the North American continent, and especially from the Rocky Mountains and the Great Lakes region. There are no easy explanations that can cover *all* these sightings.

The reports of lake monsters in North America fall into a curious pattern. Nearly all are from mountain lakes, or from the rivers and lakes connected directly with them,

which include the Great Lakes.

An apparent exception to this was a series of reports of a monster in Alkali Lake (now Walgen Lake), which lies in the grasslands of Nebraska. The first reported sighting was in the summer of 1921, when a farmer saw a creature that spouted water 15 to 20 feet (4.5 to 6 metres) high. Several other reports followed. In one incident, five witnesses were said to have seen a brownish creature 'with the shape of a huge fish'. They could not see its head or tail, but the part they could see rose about 20 inches (50 centimetres) out of the water and was 12 to 15 feet (3.5 to 4.5 metres) long. They estimated that the total length of the beast must have been 20 feet (6 metres) or more.

## Making the news

Unfortunately, these accounts all came through a journalist, John G. Maher. He was local correspondent for the *New York Herald* and, as he himself later confessed, was not above making up news when the real thing was in short supply. However, his imaginative accounts of the Alkali Lake monster created an interest that got out of hand. A local businessmen's association tried to mount an expedition to catch the monster, but were refused permission to use the lake. The monster even found its way into the material collected by a government agency, the Federal Writers' Folklore Project. Maher gave accounts of alleged sightings of the monster from earlier years. (But he did not mention that in 1889 the lake had dried up completely – without revealing any trace of a monster.)

Many of the sightings from the numerous American lakes are single reports, often from the 19th century. But a very few lakes have a long continuous history of sightings running up to the present. And after discounting journalistic invention, the accumulation of

Above: the remains of a water monster? In November 1970 this rotting carcase was washed ashore at Mann Hill Beach, Massachusetts. Long-necked and weighing between 15 and 20 tonnes, it was described as being like a camel without legs. However, it was later identified as a basking shark, which had acquired a serpent-like form when the cartilaginous parts of its body had rotted away. This, however, was a sea creature; no large animal living in the lakes is known that could give rise to the numerous reports of lake monsters

Right: the fictional monster inhabiting Lake La Metrie, about to meet its death at the hands of the US Cavalry. The saga of this relic of a prehistoric age appeared in *Pearson's Magazine* in 1899

evidence, though scattered and varied, is impressive and convincing in its totality.

One area with a long history of reports is the lake district of Wisconsin. There have been sightings in the four lakes that ring Madison, and in Waubeau, Red Cedar, Pewaukee and Elkhart Lakes. Though some of the sightings occurred in recent times it is difficult to know how much credence to place in them as they have not been properly investigated.

Of far greater interest are the reports of large water animals in the mountain states. Rumours of lake monsters in the Rockies were so common in the 19th century that they inspired sensational science fiction – such as *The monster of Lake La Metrie*, published in 1899. This story ends with a unit of the US Cavalry destroying a prehistoric plesiosaur in a remote mountain lake with a field gun.

This unlikely tale could have been based on fact, for there were many sightings of something very like a plesiosaur in several lakes. In Utah, such reports began after the Mormons had established themselves, though in the same region there had been earlier Indian legends of water creatures. The late 19th-century reports concerned Utah Lake and, especially, Bear Lake. A journalist writing in 1883 noted: 'There is abundant testimony on record of the actual existence at the present day of an immense aquatic animal of some species as yet unknown to science.'

In 1871 it was claimed that a young monster had been captured at Fish Haven, on Bear Lake – 'a creature some 20 feet [6 metres] long, which propelled itself through

the water by the action of its tail and legs.' Earlier reports spoke of a 3-foot [1-metre] neck, flippers and brown otter-like fur and a head that suggested a 'walrus without tusks'. The Shoshone Indians had said the animals used to come ashore.

These extraordinary reports faded away after the 1880s. From Payette Lake in the mountains of Idaho there were more reports in the 1930s – perhaps stimulated by the Loch Ness sensation. But in the summer of 1941 there was a sudden spate of reports. John McKay saw a large animal with a 'long dark body' and humps. A few months later a periscope-like head and neck were seen. These reports were not publicised. Then a local businessman described to the press his sighting of a 'snub-nosed crocodile' 50 feet (15 metres) long. This creature, nicknamed 'Slimy Slim', is still being reported. In June 1977 two people fishing in a boat in Cougar Bay noticed what looked like the wake of a boat – yet no boat had passed within the previous 10 minutes. Then they spotted a three-humped black object, 30 feet (9 metres) long, moving fairly fast.

Gary S. Mangiacopra, who has investigated these reports, suggests that the monster may well be some evolved form of elephant seal. This suggestion, however, scarcely accounts for the reports of humps that feature in so many of the sightings.

Reports of crocodile-like creatures have come from Folsom Lake in California, from lakes in the Trinity Alps, in the same state, and from many other places in the western states. However, Flathead Lake in Montana is the most interesting. In 1885 the captain of a lake steamer, the *U.S. Grant*, saw what he

A sturgeon (below) that came from Flathead Lake, Montana, lending colour to the theory that these fish give rise to monster reports. But this specimen was probably put into the lake (bottom right) to publicise it among local fishermen

Bottom left: the lakes of western North America. Mountain lakes seem to be the preferred haunts of giant water creatures

thought was another boat bearing down on him and then realised that it was a large whale-like animal. One of his passengers fired on it before it sank out of sight. In 1919 passengers on another boat, the *City of Polson*, saw what they thought was a log moving across the path of the ship: then they saw that it was an animal swimming away from the vessel.

During the following decades there were numerous reports, many of which were published by the editor of the *Flathead Courier*, Mr Paul Fugleberg. His enthusiasm kept the story fresh for a long while. He had a theory that the monster might be a giant sturgeon. This seems unlikely as there is no evidence that such fish have ever bred in the lake. Only *once* has a sturgeon been taken from the lake – and that may have been brought there as a stunt, to publicise the quality of the fishing.

STURGEON FISH, CAUGHT IN FLATHEAD LAKE - 5-28-55 WEIGHT 181 LBS. 1 OZ. 7½' LONG CAUGHT BY LESLIE GRIFFITH

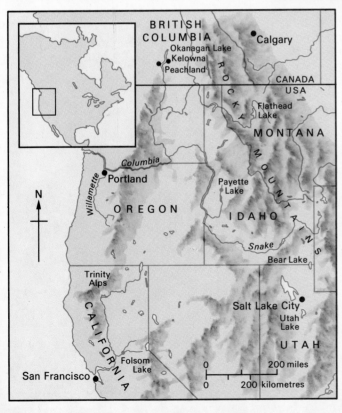

**Native peoples thought of the North American lakes as the homes of numerous divinities – including monsters. But flesh-and-blood water animals are the prizes sought by modern investigators**

CANADA AND ALASKA, lands scattered with innumerable lakes, do not lack for reports of monsters. Behind these modern reports there is a long legendary tradition among the native Eskimos and Indians.

In the late 1940s the Canadian writer Farley Mowat (then a naturalist in government service) was told about a monster called Angeoa, which had been seen in Tulemaliguak (Dubawnt Lake). His informant was an Eskimo friend, whose father and a companion had seen the creature at the end of the last century. The bones of a great beast had once been found on the shores of the lake: hence its Eskimo name, Lake of the Heaped-up Bones. As for the monster:

It was beyond the words of the people to tell you about, but my father who saw it said it was as long as twenty kayaks and broader than five. It had a fin which stood up from one end and that fin was as big as a tent. Neither my father nor Hekwaw saw its head and did not believe the beast had a head.

Terrified, the two Eskimos fled, but their kayak overturned. The informant's father survived, but his companion drowned.

This creature was doubtless related to the creature known in the Great Lakes area as Manitou Niba Nabais, the god of the waters and lakes. But these legends are scientifically relevant only as background to modern reports.

Take the case of Iliamna Lake in Alaska. This lake covers 1000 square miles (1600 square kilometres) and is said to be the seventh largest in the world. It is 90 miles (145 kilometres) long, whereas Loch Ness is only 22 miles (35 kilometres) long. In the scattered hamlets around the shores there are legends of the creature snatching children and caribou and biting through canoes.

In 1971 it was reported that the monster broke up the winter ice at Kokhanok, a small village on the south-eastern shore. Children sketched it before it disappeared. Susie Noatak drew it with 'an eye below his mouth'; John Nelson junior drew it as some kind of giant whale or sturgeon, trailing long tendrils. Some of the local game guards are convinced the creature is indeed a large sturgeon. A US Geological Survey worker saw two creatures together. In the mid 1960s some NASA astronauts flying an aircraft over the lake saw great shadows moving in the water. They swooped down over the lake and the shapes vanished. An old Indian told Reuben Gaines, a television personality and writer, that he saw someone shrivel up and die after seeing the lake monster. Some Indians refused to go out in red-bottomed boats, for red annoyed the monster.

Above: the Texas oil magnate Tom Slick, a keen monster hunter. He mounted an expedition to find the legendary monster of Iliamna Lake in Alaska, but failed in his quest. He is pictured here after a fruitless search for the Yeti in the Himalayas

Right: Simcoe Lake, Ontario, reputedly the home of a monster (inset) variously dubbed Igopogo and Kempenfelt Kelly. Reports of the monster go back to the 19th century

Centre right: the classic photograph of Manipogo, the monster of Lake Manitoba, taken on 12 August 1962. The two fishermen who took the picture saw what they 'believed to be a large black snake or eel . . . which was swimming with a ripple action'. They estimated that the hump was about 2 feet (60 centimetres) long. Their boat had an outboard motor, but they were unable to keep up with the creature and it escaped from them

Far right: the lakes north of Winnipeg, Manitoba. The best-known of the monsters reported from this area is Manipogo, reputed to dwell in Lake Manitoba

**Coming up**

A giant sturgeon, or some type of whale? These were the questions to which a renowned Texas oilman, Tom Slick, addressed himself when he investigated, with the help of Commander Stanley Lee, the reports that US Navy airmen had seen the creature. But they failed to find any large animal. In 1966 a New York photographer, Leonard Rue, tried again to see if there was anything in the legends, and had equal lack of success. Local people resent the fact that many expeditions go to Loch Ness, but so few to Alaska.

But Iliamna Lake is a bleak place. Other more favoured lakes have received some investigation. In Simcoe Lake, Ontario, which is near Toronto, a creature called Igopogo has been searched for by several expeditions. During the last century there were persistent reports, which were given greater plausibility by an Indian trapper's account in 1952. In 1963 a creature 'charcoal-coloured, 30 to 70 feet [9 to 21 metres] long and with dorsal fins' was seen by a minister, an undertaker and their families. It has been described by others as a dog-faced animal with a neck the diameter of a stove pipe.

Its supposed lair was in Kempenfelt Bay and it was dubbed 'Kempenfelt Kelly' for that reason. The bay was fouled by a million gallons (4.5 million litres) of raw sewage in July 1980. But a few days later the creature was seen in Cook's Bay by John Bergeron and his Uncle Gaston. It had a head two and half times the size of a human's, a camel's hump, and a tail 7 feet (2.1 metres) long. 'There it was, with eyes as big as a cow's, jumping in the water for several minutes.' Luckily the monster had escaped the pollution.

There were also early reports about a monster in Lake Ontario. More recent reports seem to confirm this. And there was another in the nearby Deschênes Lake in 1880 – part of its hairy hide was caught up in a propeller. A 'crocodile' stirred up New Hamburg, Ontario, in 1953. The local Mountie took a shot at it. Other monsters are said to live in some of the remote lakes further north.

Further west, beyond the Great Lakes, lie the numerous lakes of Manitoba. A series of connected lakes lies north of Winnipeg: Lakes Winnipeg, Manitoba, Winnipegosis and Dauphin. Lake Winnipeg alone covers 124 square miles (300 square kilometres).

The first report was from Lake Manitoba in 1908. A year later a trapper saw a huge creature swimming at about 2 miles per hour (3 km/h). It had a dark upper surface, which glistened, and its body projected 4 feet (1.2 metres) out of the water.

Other reports followed over the years. In

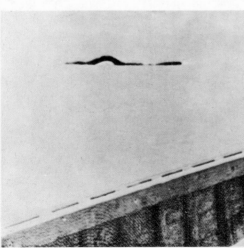

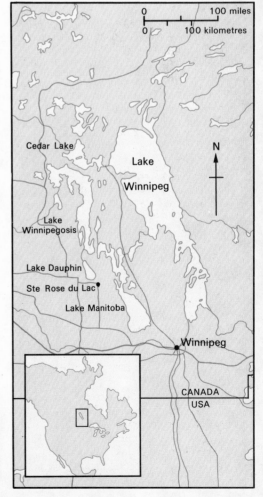

1957 two men, Louis Belcher and Eddie Nipanik, saw a serpent-like monster in Lake Manitoba. Their reports and others that year – one witness spoke of hearing 'a bellow like a goods train whistle' – gave rise to a great deal of local concern. The provincial government sent in a team to search the lake for the monster, now dubbed 'Manipogo'. The Minister of Industry and Commerce said the safety and prosperity of Lake Manitoba might depend on the expedition. But the team failed to find any animal large enough to pose any kind of threat, to fishermen or to other lake users.

But still the reports came in. In the summer of 1960 a full-scale, if short-lived, scientific investigation was set up. On 12 August 1962 two fishermen, Richard Vincent and John Konefell, snapped what they reported was Manipogo. A Winnipeg zoologist, Dr James A. Macleod, said of the shallow-humped object in the picture: 'If that isn't the monster, I'd like to know what the deuce it is.'

These reports, though numerous, are far exceeded in volume by the evidence from Okanagan Lake concerning the monster there, the great Ogopogo. Already the subject of two books, Ogopogo has been called the Nessie of North America. But Nessie might better be called the Ogopogo of Scotland, because reports of the Canadian monster go back to 1850 – long before the notoriety of Nessie.

Okanagan is a long, deep mountain lake, running north to south in the pleasant fruit-growing territory of southern British Columbia. The details of innumerable reports give a picture of a large, dark-coloured creature with a long neck and humped back. Some sample reports show up the striking similarities.

In July 1890, Captain Thomas Shorts on the steamer *Jubilee* saw an animal off Squally Point, some 15 feet (5 metres) long, with a ram-like head and the Sun shining through its fins. This was one of the first reports;

there were another half dozen before 1925, when the rumour of the monster was taken up by a Vancouver paper and its modern history began. The idea, then popular, that the creature was a giant sturgeon was contradicted by many reports of a long-necked animal.

A classic case was the sighting in July 1959 by Dick Miller (the editor of the *Vernon Advertiser*) and his wife. Three days later he published his own account of the creature:

Returning from a cruise down the Okanagan Lake, travelling at 10 miles an hour [16 km/h], I noticed, about 250 feet [75 metres] in our wake, what appeared to be the serpent. On picking up the field glasses my thoughts were verified. It was Ogopogo and it was travelling a great deal faster than we were. I would judge around 15 to 17 miles an hour [24 to 27 km/h]. The head was about 9 inches [23 centimetres] above the water. The head was definitely snake-like with a blunt nose. . . . [They turned the boat round to approach the creature.] Our excitement was short-lived. We watched for

Above: Arlene B. Gaal, who has made Ogopogo her special study. In 1981 she photographed the monster, she believes

Right: Ogopogo, as filmed by Art Folden in August 1968. When the moving picture is viewed, three humps are apparent here

Above right: the creature leaves a wake as it moves off at high speed

Below: this plaque reflects the importance of Ogopogo to local tourism

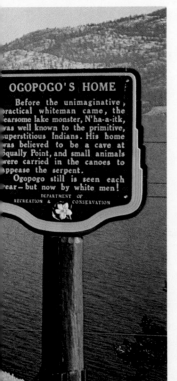

about three minutes, as Ogie did not appear to like the boat coming on him broadside, very gracefully reduced the five humps which were so plainly visible, lowered his head and gradually submerged. At no time was the tail visible. The family's version of the colour is very dark greenish. . . . This sea serpent glides gracefully in a smooth motion (without snake-like undulations sideways). This would lead one to believe that in between the humps it possibly has some type of fin, which it works together or possibly individually to control direction.

Ogopogo has been the subject of a much disputed ciné film, taken by Art Folden in August 1968. He and his wife were driving back to their home in Chase, along the shores of the lake. At a point on Highway 97, just south of the town of Peachland, and about 300 yards (300 metres) from the lake, they saw something large moving through the water.

Art Folden, as luck would have it, was equipped with an 8-millimetre ciné camera, loaded with colour film and fitted with a telephoto lens. There was a short run of film left over from his coverage of the day's family outing. Focusing on the bay below he exposed a minute of film in short bursts, photographing the object only when it was visible on the surface.

Was Canada's most celebrated monster 'in the can' at last? Reluctant to expose himself to publicity, Folden kept quiet about the film, showing it only at home to his friends and relatives. A year later, in late 1969, his brother-in-law persuaded him to show the film publicly. When it was screened in February 1970 it caused a sensation. There then followed a spate of well-authenticated reports of sightings, but the film itself was disputed.

Pine trees in the foreground in some shots suggested that the object was about 60 feet (18 metres) long – the size of a canal barge. It was some 3 feet (1 metre) across. It was clearly moving very fast with a definite wake. Some viewers thought they could make out a head and tail. Many local people were unconvinced, however. But Arlene Gaal, a local writer and author of a book dealing with the story of the Okanagan monster, investigated the site where the film was made, and became convinced that Art Folden's film showed some 'unusual form of life' in the deep waters of the lake.

In 1967 a black and white photograph, ostensibly showing Ogopogo, was discovered in the files of Kelowna Chamber of Commerce. The man who took it did not want any publicity for himself, even when the photograph was published in the local paper. He claimed to have seen the hump-backed creature in a small bay near Kelowna Bridge, but it had disappeared by the time he took the photograph. The picture probably shows 'windrows' – patterns on the surface created by the wind, and giving the appearance of humps.

Every year more reports came in. On 3 August 1976 a set of five photographs was taken by Ed Fletcher of Vancouver. For several hours that day he and his party chased Ogopogo back and forth while he took his series of colour photographs. These do indeed show a long, humped object moving through the water. Was it the monster? Or merely an effect of standing waves? (These are the stationary or slow-moving waves created where ordinary waves, travelling in different directions, overlap.) The witnesses had no doubts: they spoke of seeing a head and 'two things standing up from the head like the ears of a Dobermann pinscher'.

If any place provides ideal conditions for investigating reports of lake monsters it is Okanagan Lake. But, as we shall see, only a few intrepid scientists and laymen have taken up the challenge they present.

**Explanations for the reported sightings of monsters in the North American lakes are nearly as numerous as the reports themselves. The theory that an unknown species of water animal is awaiting discovery is still a prime contender**

WHILE MONSTER-HUNTING expeditions to Loch Ness have received enormous publicity, far less is heard of the research carried out on North American lakes. Predictably, 'official' zoologists and fisheries officials have tended to dismiss reports of monsters; but occasionally they have been more open-minded and have thrown resources into the search for unknown creatures.

Reports of strange animals in Lake Pohenegamook, in Quebec, started as long ago as 1874, and there was another spate of sightings in the 1920s. In 1957 Dr Vadim Vladikov, Director of the Quebec Department of Game and Fisheries, launched an investigation into the monster, which came to be called Ponik, or the Pohenegamook Sea Cow. According to descriptions given to Dr Vladikov, Ponik was:

an animal between 12 and 18 feet [3.5 and 5.5 metres] long, brown or black in colour, with a round black back 2 or 3 feet [60 or 90 centimetres] wide, and a sawtooth fin down the centre. Any time anyone approaches close, the animal slithers away and sinks below the lake's surface.

Dr Vladikov, however, could find no tangible evidence of the creature. In the mid 1970s it was again investigated, this time by an expedition set up by an American organisation, the Society for the Investigation of the Unexplained. For 10 days three divers searched for the animal with the aid of sonar,

Above: the monster of Lake Champlain, on the border between Canada and the United States. The length of body seen above the water has been reported as about 20 feet (6 metres)

Below: Lake Champlain in the grip of winter ice

and they did obtain a trace of an object about 25 feet (7.5 metres) long underneath their boat, and on film they recorded a rather murky dark shape.

Other Canadian lake monsters have been investigated by qualified scientists. For many years the lakes north of Winnipeg have produced numerous sightings of unidentified animals. Lake Manitoba has been a particularly prolific source of reports since the first in 1908, but the sightings of 1960 were astounding. On 22 July 20 people saw 'a large reptile'. Three weeks later on the same beach – now, naturally, named 'Manipogo Beach' – 17 people saw three monsters: two large ones and a smaller one.

These reports aroused the keen interest of Dr James A. Macleod, Chairman of the Zoological Department of the University of Manitoba. Dr Macleod was open-minded enough to take seriously the possibility that some prehistoric reptile did indeed survive in

# The ones that got away

the northern end of the lake. But his research was short-lived because it was hard to find the finance to back the study of such ideas.

Lake Champlain, which straddles the Canadian-American border, has been the subject of much research in recent years, and possibly our best chance of finding out what these mysterious animals are lies here. The first reliable reports came from 1819, when pioneer settlers near Port Henry, New York state, saw the creature in Bulwagga Bay. After more than a half century of silence on the subject, there was a spate of sightings in the 1870s. The creature was reported by an excursion party in Horseshoe Bay, and during the summer of 1871 by the passengers of the steamer *Curlew*. The accounts spoke of a head raised on an erect neck, leaving a wake 30 to 40 feet (9 to 12 metres) long.

These reports came to the notice of the great P.T. Barnum, who in 1873 offered a reward of $50,000 for the hide of the 'sea serpent', which was to be sent to New York's State Hall in a copper boiler. On 30 October of that year the monster was given further celebrity by Thomas Nast, the crusading cartoonist of *Harper's Weekly* (best known for his part in bringing down the corrupt Tammany politician 'Boss' Tweed). Nast delighted the lecture audience with his baroque rendering of the creature.

This was all good fun, but even Barnum's tempting prize did not produce substantial evidence. However, in July 1880 a Dr Brigham and Mr Ashley Shelters saw the animal in Missiquoi Bay, in the Canadian waters of the lake. As they afterwards told the story:

> portions of its body fully 20 feet [6 metres] in length appeared above the surface of the water. . . . [Its head was] as large as a flour barrel . . . of irregular shape . . . eyes being of greenish tinge.

Captain Mooney, sheriff of Clinton County, made a report of great interest. The animal he saw raised its head 4 or 5 feet (1.2 or 1.5 metres) out of the rough water; it was about 25 feet (7.5 metres) long and the exposed neck was 7 inches (18 centimetres) across. Mooney noted the muscles contracting in its neck, which was curved like that 'of a goose

Above: Lake Champlain's mystery creature, as photographed by Sandra Mansi in 1977. Sceptics suggest that what seem to be the head and neck are in reality the fin of a small whale, appearing above the water as the creature rolls on its side

Below: Ponik, the monster that supposedly inhabits Lake Pohenegamook in Quebec, is noteworthy for the sawtooth fin along its back. It is thought that sonar equipment detected it on one occasion

when about to take flight'.

Even more astonishing was a report of an animal hauling itself some 6 feet (2 metres) onto the shore at Cumberland Head in September 1899. It was said to be dark on top and lighter underneath – the camouflage colours one would expect for an aquatic animal.

By 1982 there were over 130 reports of the Lake Champlain monster. Of these 33 mention a long neck, the one feature that distinguishes reports of lake monsters from Loch Ness to Patagonia. It is hard to believe that any conventional explanation, such as a large fish, an otter or a seal, can account for all the details of the evidence.

Naturally, odd stories abound among the lake shore families. According to Carl Washburn – who had himself seen the monster while out fishing with his father in 1900 – 'another serpent had been caught and tied up near North Beach in Burlington'. Unfortunately, it escaped.

We owe the fact that so many reports have been preserved to the personal interest of a local journalist, Walter Hard, editor of *Vermont Life*. The part played by intelligent local editors in recording incidents such as the lake monster sightings cannot be overemphasised. One Scottish editor says her paper never publishes reports of water monsters, as a matter of policy. Fortunately, some others are more enlightened.

Extensive coverage of lake monster stories has the regrettable consequence that every possible oddity from the lake is twisted into a 'sea serpent' story. In 1945 a syndicated news

story was distributed under the headline 'Baby sea serpent taken in Vermont water – may be offspring of lake monster'. It reported that Erwin Bell of Burlington, an employee of the Champlain Transportation Company, captured a 14-inch (35-centimetre) 'reptile' in shallow water at Shelburne Bay. It resembled a small alligator, except that it had smaller jaws. Bell himself supposed that this 'baby sea serpent' was some kind of salamander – and he was probably correct.

The hero of Lake Champlain monster research is Joseph M. Zarzynski. In 1975 Zarzynski, then a 25-year-old social studies teacher, became 'almost obsessed' with the problem. From then on he and his friends made annual expeditions to the lake, following up old reports and discovering new ones. Exploration around Lake Champlain is difficult and costly. But his persistence has begun to pay off. Lacking the resources that have been expended on Loch Ness over the years, he has built up an immense dossier of reports, and has investigated the lake with great fortitude.

One thing disturbs him. He has noted that there seem to be fewer sightings of long-necked creatures in the years since 1920. The descriptions available from the early decades of this century and from the last century are also better than the later ones. The ever-increasing recreational use of the lake may be putting pressure on the monsters and gradually wiping them out, he surmises. In 1979 he appealed for protection of the creatures. In October 1980 the town trustees of Port Henry declared their waters off limits to anyone intent on harming the Champ, as the lake creature had been dubbed, and efforts were under way to get the legal protection of

Phineas T. Barnum, the great American showman, made his own contribution – of questionable value – to the study of unknown lake creatures by offering the huge sum of $50,000 for the Lake Champlain monster. He would have been content with the hide of the monster – which, fortunately, no hunter succeeded in providing

the New York state authorities.

The Zarzynski expeditions brought the Champ to the attention of newspapers and magazines all over the world, and made it almost as famous as Nessie. Then, at the end of June 1981, a colour photograph said to show the monster was published and aroused heated controversy. The photographer, Sandra Mansi, said she had taken the picture in July 1977 with a pocket camera. It showed the creature at the surface, its long neck curved back over a low humped body.

The Optical Sciences Center at the University of Arizona was asked to examine the print – the original negative had vanished. Professor B.R. Frieden, assisted by J.R. Greenwell, pronounced the print genuine. But Professor Paul Kurtz of the State University of New York, well-known as a debunker of all things mysterious and unexplained, said he thought the monster was as real as UFOs, the bigfoot – or the tooth fairy. However, another academic, Roy Mackal of Chicago University, speculated that the picture might show a zeuglodon – a primitive form of whale.

Sandra Mansi's inability to remember exactly where the photograph was taken has given ammunition to her critics. But the search for a monster in Lake Champlain goes on. Clifford Rollins of Rutland, Vermont, who considers all the fuss about monsters to be 'horse manure', has offered a reward of $500 on Champ – dead or alive. This is little enough reward for solving a centuries-old mystery – especially compared with Barnum's offer – and so far there have been no claimants.

Monsters have often been dismissed as myths, hoaxes or misperceptions. The small sample of cases briefly described in these

## A touch of the sun

An atmospheric effect that could distort ordinary objects to give rise to monster reports has been described by W.H. Lehn, a Canadian scientist. It can occur when a layer of relatively warm air lies over cold air just above the water. Light rays travelling upwards from an object in the water, such as a boulder, are then deflected downward in the transition region between the two temperature zones (below). A person at an appropriate distance will see a composite of multiple images of the object – one

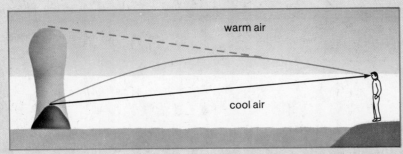

warm air

cool air

formed by light rays that have travelled in a straight line to his eye, and others formed by rays that have followed a curved path. This composite image of the object can be distorted in a vast number of different ways. One of the most common effects is to 'stretch' the image upwards, without making it correspondingly wider. The long thin shape resulting is very like many descriptions of sea serpents' necks. The object may be sufficiently distinctive to be recognisable – for example, it may be a ship. Or the atmospheric conditions may change, leaving the object in plain view. But in other cases the shifting layers of cold and warm air can create the illusion of a creature submerging and reappearing. The object may also have its own real motion: for example, a 'sea serpent' may be a killer whale, projecting its head from the water briefly – a hunting procedure that is called 'spy-hopping'. The phenomenon is, in fact, a mirage.

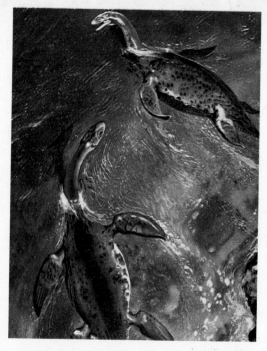

Left: two plesiosaurs of the Jurassic era. It is often suggested that some of them survived their supposed extinction and are the modern lake monsters

Below: the white whale, or beluga, which inhabits Arctic seas and rivers, and is often cited as the cause of monster sightings

therefore better able to cope with changes of water temperature.

Others have looked for less radical explanations. At Lake Flathead in Montana it has always been thought that the local monster might be a giant sturgeon. There are instances of Pacific sturgeon up to 18 feet (5.5 metres) in length; but in Russia they have been known to grow to about 26 feet (8 metres). Giant sticklebacks, manatees, white whales – these are other theories that have been proposed. And then there are the really radical theories: the suggestions that, because they have proved so elusive, like 'manimals' and giant flying creatures, they are psychic manifestations – perhaps a product of a particular witness's mind at a particular place and time.

But if the monsters exist and are of ordinary flesh and blood, then it is likely that the mystery will be solved one day, by the stranding of a carcase – or the capture of a large aquatic creature with distinctive eyes, a furry hide and a strange cry.

articles should make it clear that such wholesale dismissals are unjustified. Hoaxes and journalistic fabrication cover only a few incidents, which have been easily exposed. But we are still far from any solution to the mystery of what these creatures are.

Some reports of monsters may well have been optical illusions. Professor Waldemar H. Lehn of the University of Winnipeg has suggested that a distortion of the paths of light waves – a mirage – over the cold waters of a lake can cause ordinary objects and animals, such as a lake shore boulder, to appear greatly elongated, giving the long-necked appearance that is so typical of all monster photographs. But Dr Lehn insists that it is not the aim of his proposal 'to discredit the existence of yet unidentified animals or species, for there is impressive evidence to the contrary from sonar data and underwater photography'.

But while this may account for part of the evidence, it would be ridiculous as an explanation for the accounts of creatures 20 to 40 feet (6 to 12 metres) long, capable of hauling themselves onto the shore or making off at great speed. In many cases it is quite clear that the witnesses have seen something large, animate and terrifying.

Could it be that what they have seen is normal enough, but out of place? It has been suggested by the writer Loren Coleman that the monsters in the Californian Lake Folsom are errant crocodiles; however, a crocodile is unlikely to survive in the cold water of a mountain lake.

The same argument was brought against the suggestion that sea serpents and, by extension, lake monsters are surviving prehistoric reptiles, animals along the lines of long-necked plesiosaurs. But it has been suggested that some of the prehistoric reptiles may well have been 'warm-blooded' and

Right: a manatee, or sea cow – a plant-eating mammal confined to shallow tropical waters. If lake-dwelling cousins exist they may account for a few of the reports of monsters

# Merfolk

**Half human and half fish, mermaids and mermen have appeared many times over the centuries. But, asks PAUL BEGG, are the merfolk merely colourful figments of our imagination – or do they really exist?**

ACCORDING TO THE South African *Pretoria News* of 20 December 1977, a mermaid had been found in a storm sewer in the Limbala Stage III township, Lusaka. The reports are garbled and it is difficult to tell who saw what – and what exactly it was they saw – but it seems that the 'mermaid' was first seen by some children and, as the news spread, so a crowd gathered. One reporter was told that the creature appeared to be a 'European woman from the waist up, whilst the rest of her body was shaped like the back end of a fish, and covered with scales.'

Legends about mermaids and mermen stretch back into antiquity and can be found in the folklore of almost every nation in the world. Merfolk have been seen and vouched for down the ages by witnesses of attested integrity – and they continue to be seen today.

The earliest merman in recorded history is the fish-tailed god Ea, more familiarly known as Oannes, one of the three great gods of the Babylonians. He had dominion over

# A fishy tale

the sea and was also the god of light and wisdom, and the bringer of civilisation to his people. Originally Oannes was the god of the Akkadians, a Semitic people of the northern part of Babylonia from whom the Babylonians derived their culture, and was worshipped in Akkad as early as 5000 BC.

Almost all we know about the cult of Oannes is derived from the surviving fragments of a three-volume history of Babylonia written by Berossus, a Chaldean priest of Bel in Babylon, in the third century BC. In the 19th century, Paul Emil Botta, the French vice-consul in Mosul, Iraq, and an enthusiastic archaeologist – albeit one whose primary concern was loot – discovered a remarkable sculpture of Oannes dating from the eighth century BC, in the palace of the Assyrian king Sargon II at Khorabad, near Mosul. The sculpture, along with a rich collection of carved slabs and cuneiform inscriptions, is now held in the Louvre in Paris.

Another early fish-tailed god was Dagon of the Philistines who is mentioned in the Bible: 1 Samuel 5:1–4. The Ark of the Covenant was placed next to a statue of Dagon in a temple dedicated to Dagon in Ashod, one of the five great Philistine city states. The following day the statue was found to have 'fallen upon his face to the earth before the ark of the Lord'. Amid much consternation

and, no doubt, great fear, the people of Ashod set the statue of Dagon in its place again, but the following day it was again found fallen before the Ark of the Covenant, this time the head and the hands having broken off.

It is also probable that the wife and daughters of Oannes were fish-tailed, but the surviving representations of them are vague and it is impossible to be sure. However, no doubts surround Atargatis, sometimes known as Derceto, a Semitic Moon goddess. In his *De dea Syria* the Greek writer Lucian (*c*. AD 120–*c*. 180) described her: 'Of this Derceto likewise I saw in Phoenicia a drawing in which she is represented in a curious form; for in the upper half she is a woman, but from the waist to the lower extremities runs in the tail of a fish.'

Fish-tailed deities can be found in almost every culture of the ancient world but by medieval times they had become humanoid sea-dwellers. One of the most important scientific influences on the Middle Ages was Pliny the Elder (AD 23–79), a Roman administrator and encyclopedic writer who died in the eruption of Vesuvius that destroyed Pompeii (and whose 15th-century statue outside Como Cathedral looks disconcertingly like Harpo Marx). As far as medieval scholars were concerned, if Pliny said that something was so then it was

Top left: the 'Fejee mermaid' that was the star attraction of Phineas T. Barnum's touring show in 1842. Barnum, a cynical American showman who coined the phrase 'every crowd has a silver lining', advertised the creature with posters depicting voluptuous mermaids, similar to the painting by Waterhouse (top). The 'mermaid' was perhaps a freak fish

undeniably so. Of mermaids, Pliny wrote:

I am able to bring forth for mine authors divers knights of Rome . . . who testifie that in the coast of the Spanish Ocean neere unto Gades, they have seen a Mere-man, in every respect resembling a man as perfectly in all parts of the bodie as might bee. . . .

Why, if the man so perfectly resembled a human, the 'divers knights of Rome' thought they had seen a *mer*man is not clear, but Pliny was convinced that merfolk were real and that they were seen regularly.

Tales of merfolk proliferated and were, oddly, encouraged by the Church, which found it politic to adapt ancient heathen legends to its own purpose. Mermaids were included in bestiaries, and carvings of them were featured in many churches and cathedrals. A fine example of a mermaid carving can

Above: the mermaid who is said to have abducted one Mathy Trewhella, carved for posterity on a pew in the church at Zennor, Cornwall. The carving is about 600 years old, but the legend may be considerably older

Left: mermaids, mermen and mer-children disport themselves in the turbulent sea

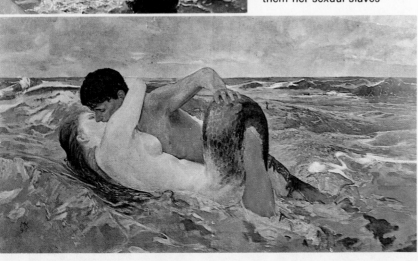

Below: the mermaid as erotic fantasy figure. She was widely believed to prey on drowning sailors, making them her sexual slaves

be seen in the church at Zennor, Cornwall, on a bench end. It is thought to be about 600 years old and is associated with the legend of Mathy Trewhella, the son of the churchwarden, who one day inexplicably disappeared. Years later a sea captain arrived at St Ives and told how he had anchored off Pendower Cave and seen a mermaid who had said to him: 'Your anchor is blocking our cave and Mathy and our children are trapped inside.' For the people of Zennor the mystery of Mathy's disappearance was explained.

On the whole, mermaids were not a sight to be relished. Their beautiful song, it was said, had captivated many a ship's crew and, like the fabled sirens, lured vessels to grief on dangerous rocks.

## When mermaids surface

In the late Elizabethan, early Jacobean age belief in the mermaid waxed and waned. Men such as Frances Bacon and John Donne gave rational explanations for many natural phenomena, including the mermaid – yet it was also a time of blossoming maritime travel and some of the great seamen of the age told of personal encounters with merfolk. In 1608 Henry Hudson, the navigator and explorer (after whom the Hudson Bay territories are named), made the following matter-of-fact entry in his log:

This morning, one of our companie looking over boord saw a Mermaid, and calling up some of the companie to see her, one more came up, and by that time she was come close to the ship's side, looking earnestly on the men: a little after, a Sea came and overturned her: From the Navill upward, her back and breasts were like a womans (as they say that saw her) her body as big as one of us; her skin very white; and long haire hanging down behinde, of colour blacke; in her going downe they saw her tayle, which was like the tayle of a Porposse, and speckled like a Macrell. Their names that saw her were Thomas Hilles and Robert Raynar.

Hudson was a very experienced seaman who surely knew the calibre of his men and presumably would not have bothered to record a blatant hoax. Also, the report itself shows that his men were familiar with the creatures of the sea and were of the opinion that this creature was exceptional – which, if their description is accurate, indeed it was.

But the great age for mermaids was the 19th century. More mermaids were faked and displayed to awed crowds at fairs and exhibitions than at any other time. It was also the period in which several remarkable sightings were reported, including two of the best authenticated on record.

On 8 September 1809 *The Times* published the following letter from one William Munro:

About twelve years ago when I was Parochial Schoolmaster at Reay

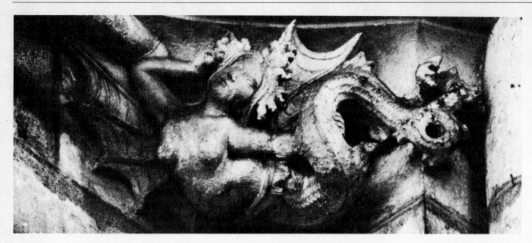

Left: a mermaid cornice decoration in Sens Cathedral, France

Below: the sirens attempt to lure Ulysses and his crew to their doom with their irresistible singing. Seen here as mermaids, they are more often thought of as half woman, half bird (below right)

Bottom: a predatory mermaid seizes a sailor and carries him off to her lair

[Scotland], in the course of my walking on the shore at Sandside Bay, being a fine warm day in summer, I was induced to extend my walk towards Sandside Head, when my attention was arrested by the appearance of a figure resembling an unclothed human female, sitting on a rock extending into the sea, and apparently in the action of combing its hair, which flowed around its shoulders, and of a light brown colour. The resemblance which the figure bore to its prototype in all its visible parts was so striking, that had not the rock on which it was sitting been dangerous for bathing, I would have been constrained to have regarded it as really a human form, and to an eye unaccustomed to the situation, it most undoubtedly appeared as such. The head was covered with hair of the colour above mentioned and shaded on the crown, the forehead round, the face plump, the cheeks ruddy, the eyes blue, the mouth and lips of natural form, resembling those of a man; the teeth I could not discover, as the mouth was shut; the breasts and abdomen, the arms and fingers of the size of a full-grown body of the human species, the fingers, from the action in which the hands were employed, did not appear to be webbed, but to this I am not positive. It remained on the rock three or four minutes after I observed it, and was exercised during that period in combing its hair, which was long and thick, and of which it appeared proud, and then dropped into the sea. . . .

Whatever it was that William Munro saw and described in such detail, he was not alone, for he adds that several people 'whose veracity I never heard disputed' had claimed to have seen the mermaid, but until he had seen it himself he 'was not disposed to credit their testimony'. But, as they say, seeing is believing.

In about 1830 inhabitants of Benbecula, in the Hebrides, saw a young mermaid playing happily in the sea. A few men tried to swim out and capture her, but she easily outswam

them. Then a little boy threw stones at her, one of which struck the mermaid and she swam away. A few days later, about 2 miles (3 kilometres) from where she was first seen, the corpse of the little mermaid was washed ashore. The tiny, forlorn body brought crowds to the beach and after the corpse had been subjected to a detailed examination it was said that:

the upper part of the creature was about the size of a well-fed child of three or four years of age; with an abnormally developed breast. The hair was long, dark and glossy; while the skin was white, soft and tender. The lower part of the body was like a salmon, but without scales.

Among the many people who viewed the tiny corpse was Duncan Shaw, factor (land agent) for Clanranald, baron-bailie and sheriff of the district. He ordered that a coffin and shroud be made for the mermaid and that she be peaceably laid to rest.

Of the many faked merfolk of this period, only one or two need be mentioned to

Below right: the Reverend
Robert S. Hawker, who, in
his youth, impersonated a
mermaid off the shore of
Bude, Cornwall. For several
nights he draped himself
over the rocks, with plaited
seaweed for hair and oilskins
wrapped round his legs, and
sang off-key. The citizens of
Bude flocked to see the
'mermaid' but, tiring of his
joke, Hawker launched into
God save the King and dived
into the sea – his mermaid
days over

illustrate the ingenuity of the fakes and the fakers. A famous example is recounted in *The vicar of Morwenstow* by Sabine Baring-Gould. The vicar in question was the eccentric Robert S. Hawker who, for reasons best known to himself, in July 1825 or 1826 impersonated a mermaid off the shore of Bude in Cornwall. When the Moon was full he swam or rowed to a rock not far from the shore and there donned a wig made from plaited seaweed, wrapped oilskins around his legs and, naked from the waist upwards, sang – far from melodiously – until observed from the shore. When the news of the mermaid spread throughout Bude people flocked to see it, and Hawker repeated his performance.

Mermaids have continued to be seen in more recent years. One was seen in 1947 by a fisherman on the Hebridean island of Muck. She was sitting on a floating herring box (used to preserve live lobsters) combing her hair. As soon as she realised she was being observed she plunged into the sea. Until his death in the late 1950s the fisherman could not be persuaded to believe that he had not seen a mermaid.

In 1978, a Filipino fisherman, 41-year-old Jacinto Fatalvero, not only saw a mermaid one moonlit night but was helped by her to secure a bountiful catch. Little more is known, however, because having told his story, Fatalvero became the butt of jokes, the

After several appearances Hawker, having tired of his joke – and his voice a little hoarse – gave an unmistakable rendition of *God save the King* and plunged into the sea – never to appear (as a mermaid) again.

Phineas T. Barnum (1810–1891), the great American showman to whom are attributed two telling statements – 'There's one [a sucker] born every minute' and 'Every crowd has a silver lining' – bought a mermaid that he had seen being shown at a shilling a time in Watson's Coffee House in London. It was a dreadful, shrivelled-up thing – probably a freak fish – but Barnum added it to the curiosities he had gathered for his 'Greatest Show on Earth'. His trick, however, was to hang up outside his 'mermaid' sideshow an eye-catching picture of three beautiful women frolicking in an underwater cavern; under this he had a notice that read: 'A Mermaid is added to the museum – no extra charge.' Drawn by the picture and the implication of what would be seen within, many thousands of people paid their admission fee and went to see this spectacle. As Barnum said, if the shrivelled-up 'mermaid' did not meet with their expectations, the rest of the exhibits were worth the money.

object of derision – and, inevitably, hounded by the media. Understandably he refused to say another word.

It is widely accepted that the mermaid legend sprang from the misidentification of two aquatic mammals, the manatee and dugong, and possibly seals. Obviously many reports can be thus explained, but does this explanation satisfactorily account for what was seen by Henry Hudson's sailors in 1608 or for the mermaid seen by the schoolmaster William Munro? Were these and other similar sightings sea-mammals or mermaids?

One suggestion, perhaps slightly tongue in cheek, is that the merfolk are real, the descendants of our distant ancestors who came ashore from the sea. The merfolk, of course, are descended from those ancestors who either stayed in the sea or chose to return to it. Human embryos have gills that usually disappear before birth, but some babies are born with them and they have to be removed surgically.

But, whatever she is, the mermaid has a long history of sightings and continues to be seen. For this we should be thankful; the romance and folklore of the sea would be all the poorer without her.

Loch Ness Monster

**Local legends have long told of mysterious creatures living deep in the dark and brooding waters of Loch Ness. ADRIAN SHINE, director of a research project on Loch Ness, gives the background to the story**

# Rumours, legends and glimpses

THE WORLD has fewer and fewer unexplored regions – hostile or inaccessible regions such as jungles, mountain ranges, remote islands or the depths of seas or inland waters. But these are the places where any remaining unknown creatures of our Earth are likely to be found.

A scientist on the trail of an unknown animal must have a receptive ear to the observations of any people living nearby. Proof of its existence comes with verifiable sightings supported by scientific evidence. Although sceptics will dismiss out of hand local tales, folklore and legend, these can often only be exposed as true or false after painstaking research and documentation. In some cases this has been carried out successfully and 'monsters' have been identified as genuine living creatures.

Man's curiosity about the more inaccessible corners of the Earth has led to some startling discoveries. Only recently the impenetrable forests of the Congo revealed the mountain gorilla, the world's largest ape, and 'an antelope with the head of a giraffe and the hindquarters of a zebra' was identified as a species now known as the okapi. Another weird creature, also discovered this century, is the so-called Komodo dragon, which inhabits the remoter islands of Indonesia.

Situated in the Great Glen, a tear in the Earth's surface cutting across the centre of Scotland, Loch Ness is a relatively unexplored region, as impenetrable and hostile to man as any mountain or jungle. At its deepest point there is possibly more than

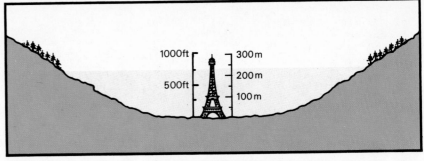

985 feet (3000 metres) of water; it stretches over a length of nearly 22 miles (35 kilometres); and because of the fine deposits of peat in the water, underwater visibility is very poor. Investigation of an area such as this requires more than human willpower or physical prowess: only the most sophisticated technological aids will – perhaps – finally unravel the mysteries of this, the largest body of fresh water in Britain.

Scientific interest in the dark depths of the sea was sparked off when commercial requirements of laying telegraph cable in the 1850s provided the stimulus and the means. Until a severed cable encrusted with animal life was raised from a depth of 6000 feet (1830 metres), it was commonly thought that all life ceased below 1800 feet (550 metres).

Britain, as the leading maritime nation, was quick to take the lead in oceanography with the dispatch of the *Challenger* expedition; this spent five years, between 1871 and 1876, dredging and sounding waters around the world. There was still, however, a

Top: the eerie beauty of Loch Ness at dawn

Above: in 1968 a submarine allegedly dived to a depth of 820 feet (250 metres) in Loch Ness; the official estimate of the phenomenal depth of the loch is 754 feet (230 metres), although other sources claim it is as much as 975 feet (297 metres) deep. The loch is less than 1 mile (1.6 kilometres) wide, and the sides plunge unusually steeply from the shore. But perhaps the most astounding feature of the loch is the sheer volume of water it contains – large enough to hold the population of the world, the loch has plenty of room for unknown creatures

Above: Komodo dragons, creatures so strange no one believed rumours of their existence until they were discovered earlier this century on a remote Indonesian island

Right: an ornate sea-dragon figurehead from a 9th-century Viking burial ship. Norse and Celtic mythologies are full of legends about the sea serpents of the seas of northern Europe

Below: a 'gigantic sea saurian' from a 19th-century English zoological work. The book contains a number of contemporary accounts of sightings of sea serpents

great reluctance to explore the freshwater world and the leader of that expedition, John Murray, had to launch a private venture to make the first study of British fresh water. This bathymetric survey of the Scottish lochs was mainly a sounding excercise that revealed the great depths of these land-locked waters.

The largest Scottish lochs are remarkable not only for their volume but for their depth, which often exceeds that of the sea surrounding our shores. Loch Morar, for example, is over 1000 feet (305 metres) deep – greater than the height of the Eiffel Tower in Paris.

The Scottish lochs all originate from the same period as the fjord-like lakes of Scandinavia and Ireland. Glaciers from successive Ice Ages deepened existing valleys, including the Great Glen fault line of Loch Ness, until about 10,000 years ago, when the ice retreated for the last time. For a while some of the lochs remained open to the sea, which had risen slightly owing to the water released by the melting ice. Then, relieved of the weight of the ice, the land rose steadily and the surface of Loch Ness, for example, now lies about 52 feet (16 metres) above sea level.

Because of the connection between these waters and the sea, it is interesting to recall some 'sea monster' tales that bear certain similarities to the 'monsters' mentioned in eyewitness accounts at Loch Ness.

### Serpents of the sagas

Ever since the prows of the Vikings' long-ships bore the Sea Dragon as a figurehead, Norse and Celtic folklore has been full of references to a long-necked, hump-backed creature of the northern waters. Bishop Erik Pontoppidan of Bergen, in his *Natural history of Norway,* published in 1752, made reference to two sea monsters seen occasionally off the coast of Norway. The first was the great kraken, the subject of mythology and fisherman's tales – 'round, flat and full of arms'. The giant squid was not recognised by scientists as the origin of the kraken legend until the 1870s, when carcases of this species were washed ashore in Newfoundland.

This coincided with the dispatch of the *Challenger* expedition and an increasing awareness of the possibilities of discovery in the oceans of the world. In 1852 a French scientist had pronounced similar remains to be a vegetable – and the existence of such an animal to be 'a contradiction of the great laws of harmony and equilibrium that have sovereign rule over living nature as well as senseless and inert matter'. Science is often dogmatic when discussing subjects it is not equipped to investigate.

The second of Pontoppidan's 'mythical' creatures was the Soe-Orm – or sea snake. The most famous of the reports he collected was that of Lorenz von Ferry, Royal Commander and Pilot General of Bergen; this provided the classic 'sea serpent' impression

of a snake-like creature, but with vertical undulations. This creature was sighted near Molde, in Norway, as von Ferry's vessel was being rowed – probably due to lack of wind – on a very calm, hot day late in August 1746. Von Ferry was reading a book when he noticed the helmsman was off course; he was informed by members of the crew that they were attempting to avoid a sea serpent ahead. He ordered them to close in on it since, despite rumours, he had hitherto doubted its existence.

## Sea-serpents ahead!

The grey-coloured head of the creature was held nearly a yard from the surface of the water and resembled that of a horse with a white mane. It had large eyes and mouth and seven or eight 'folds or coils' (possibly humps) were visible about 2 feet (60 centimetres) apart. When von Ferry fired at the creature it dived. For Pontoppidan's benefit, von Ferry later ordered two of his seamen to give sworn testimonies before a public court in Bergen. Pontoppidan would 'not entirely disbelieve what is related of the water snakes found in freshwater lakes'.

In Scandinavia many lakes have traditions of animals occasionally surfacing; these include Lake Suldal and Lake Storsjö, where implements made at the end of the 19th century to catch the 'animal' can still be seen. Similar stories involve Lake Okanagan in North America, the Lagerflot in Iceland and the Connemara loughs in Ireland which are inhabited by the pooka, kelpie or *each uisge* – 'water-horse' in Gaelic.

The kelpie and water-horse appear in the folklore of the Scottish Highlands. Strangely, however, although the first written account of a water monster in the River Ness concerns an incident in AD 565, no particular importance was given to reports from Loch Ness until quite recently. That first account

Above: a sea-serpent from Konrad von Gerner's *Fischbuch* of 1598. At that time it was still commonly believed that monsters inhabiting the depths of the seas could be a hazard to shipping

Left: the kelpie, the malignant water-sprite of the Scottish lochs, which was said to lurk by the waterside, disguised as a horse, waiting for human victims. Some of the people who live near Loch Ness can remember, as children, being told not to bathe in the loch for fear of the kelpie

was drawn from St Adaman's *Life of St Columba*, which talked of 'the driving away of a certain water monster by the virtue of prayer of the holy man'.

Appearances of this kind were – and to some extent still are – regarded with superstitious reticence as ill omens. 'Who has not heard of the Mhorag?' wrote James Mac-Donald at the turn of this century. 'The Mhorag as a rule only shows herself on Loch Morar whenever a member of a certain clan is about to die . . . the Mhorag detaches herself upon the surface in three distinct portions, one portion representing death, another a coffin, and a third a grave.'

It was most unlikely that this sort of tale would be passed on in the 19th century by the local highlanders to the culturally and socially removed gentlemen from England, who visited during the shooting season; this makes the account in Lord Malmesbury's memoirs all the more significant.

Left: Lord Malmesbury (1807–1889) who included in his *Memoirs of an ex-minister* an account of two sightings by his stalker, John Stewart, of a monster, known as the Lake Horse, in Loch Arkaig. He commented that the Highlanders were frightened of the creature, believing there to be 'something diabolical in its nature'

October 3rd 1857 – This morning my stalker and his boy gave me an account of a mysterious creature, which they say exists in Loch Arkaig, and which they call the Lake Horse. It is the same animal of which one has occasionally read accounts in newspapers as having been seen in the Highland lochs, and on the existence of which in Loch Assynt the late Lord Ellesmere wrote an interesting article. . . .

My stalker, John Stewart, at Achnacarry, has seen it twice, and both times at sunrise in summer on a bright sunny day, when there was not a ripple on the water. The creature was basking on the surface; he only saw the head and the hindquarters, proving that its back was hollow, which is not the shape of any fish or of a seal. Its head resembled that of a horse.

Lord Malmesbury commented that 'the Highlanders are very superstitious about this creature . . . and I believe they think it has something diabolical in its nature'.

Much more recently, the author Gavin Maxwell, who chose to exile himself on the west coast of Scotland, gave several accounts of similar creatures seen by friends and employees both in the sea and the sea lochs. These accounts come from skilled seamen with a lifetime's knowledge of the wildlife of the west coast.

Along with all the stories from other lochs, there have always been reports from Loch Ness. Some residents of the area can remember, as children, being told not to bathe in the loch for fear of the kelpie. But the loch really came to the public's notice only after 1933; in that year a road was blasted along the north shore and trees and undergrowth cut down to give a better view of the massive expanse of water. Among the more obvious effects of this development was the influx of visitors to the area – and so the 'sightings' of the Loch Ness 'monster' increased dramatically. The first widely publicised sighting was made on 14 April 1933 by Mr and Mrs Mackay and reported in the *Inverness Courier*. 'The creature disported itself for fully a minute, its body resembling that of a whale.' This sighting was swiftly followed by others – and so Loch Ness became a sensation throughout the world.

By now scientists had started to take an interest in freshwater biology, with the first British station beginning studies of microscopic animals and plants in Lake Windermere using primitive equipment. It was a decade before the development of sonar equipment and the aqualung would provide the means scientists needed to begin a systematic investigation of Loch Ness, and another three before advanced underwater camera techniques would make it possible to attempt to photograph the creature that is rumoured to live in the dark, peat-stained waters of the mysterious loch.

Below: a simplified distribution map of the recorded sightings of the Loch Ness monster. The monster is most often seen near the mouths of rivers

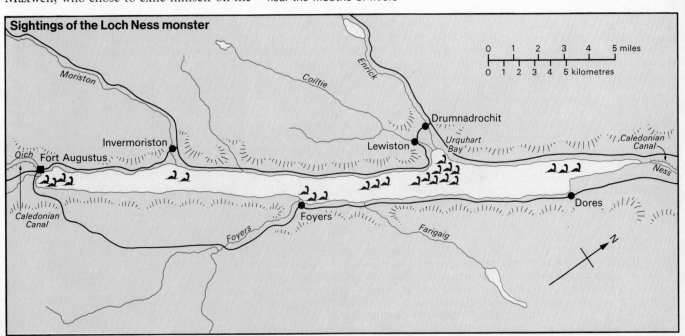

**Sightings of the Loch Ness monster**

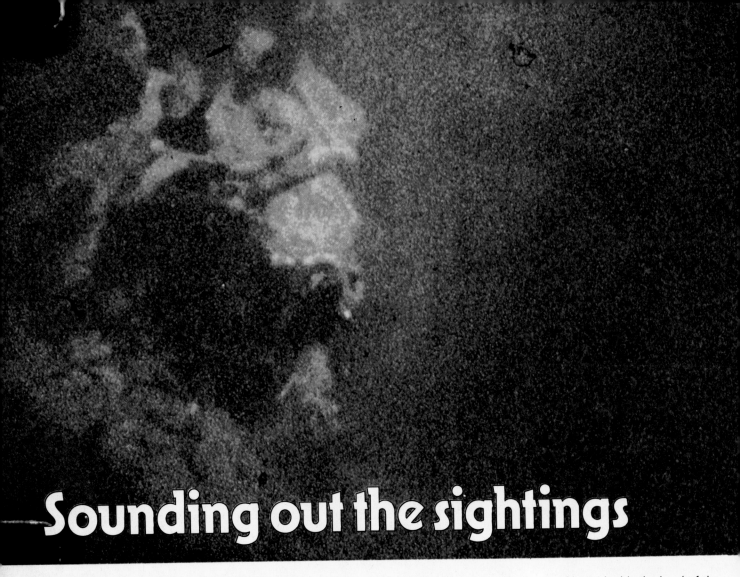

# Sounding out the sightings

**Ever since the 1930s people have been attempting to capture the Loch Ness monster on film. The archives are full of alleged photographic evidence of the existence of the monster – but how much of it is genuine? And what does it tell us about the monster?**

THE EXPLOSION of interest in what may or may not lurk in the dark depths of Loch Ness was sparked off by the Mackay sighting on 14 April 1933. Since then the volume of evidence has grown steadily – there were 50 other sightings in that year alone – and has been sustained ever since with many more sightings, photographs, films and other evidence as attempts have been made to investigate the 'monster'.

In addition to the better view afforded by tree-felling on the north side of the loch, press interest led to many sightings being documented; the two factors together could account for the apparent suddenness of the phenomenon. Once Loch Ness was publicly known to contain a mystery, people would obviously be on the lookout for any signs of the unusual and, by the same token, the interest would induce strong expectation and powerful suggestion.

The major difficulty in evaluating eyewitness accounts and evidence is one of subjectivity. An honest man may easily be mistaken or fooled; a dishonest one is quite likely to give a good impression; and an educated one may be imaginative. The fact is that without very specific experience, it is extremely difficult to judge time, size, distance or speed with any accuracy, especially over water. By pressing a witness to commit himself to just such details, the investigator is inadvertently contriving to make an honest man appear a liar or fool. So it is impossible to construct a particularly accurate picture of what has been seen by using this kind of material.

The loch itself presents problems because it plays tricks on the eyes. It is a large mass of water sometimes completely calm in a way that the sea, for example, rarely is, and its high shorelines cast deep shadows and reflections. In these conditions you can get a visual impression totally out of proportion to the actual cause – of small animals, water birds, boat wakes and wind. The wakes from boats passing through the loch, for example, can be reflected from the shores to form a standing wave in the centre of the loch after the particular boat has passed out of sight.

Despite these problems, thousands of

Above: is this the head of the Loch Ness monster? This photograph was taken, using an underwater camera, by Dr Robert Rines of the Academy of Applied Science, Massachusetts Institute of Technology, USA, on 20 June 1975. Although the peaty waters of the bottom of the loch make it difficult to identify what the photograph represents, it has been argued that the symmetry of the object shows it is animate; on the other hand, many experts hold that the photograph shows merely the bottom of the loch

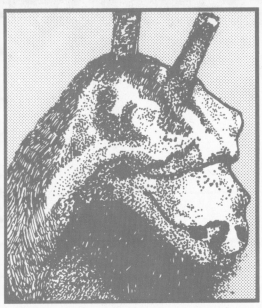

Left: an artist's impression of the object in Dr Robert Rines's photograph. Some people believe the horns may be used by the monster as snorkel tubes to enable it to breathe without surfacing

Below: from the series of underwater photographs taken by Dr Robert Rines (see also page 190), an artist was able to build up this picture of what the Loch Ness monster might look like. It shows the long neck, small head and flippers mentioned in so many reports of sightings

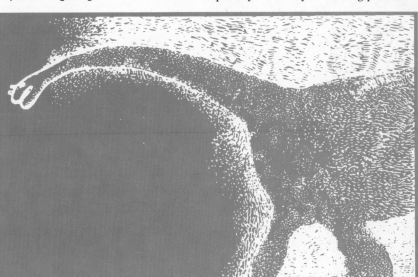

Besides eyewitness evidence, there are the photographic records of surfacings. Although the photographic image may appear irrefutable, and may be seen to present measurable evidence that can be independently assessed, the limitations of the lens in fact make any such assessment very difficult. Photographs taken with ordinary equipment give far less information than the naked eye – and, sadly, the photographic print process is very easy to manipulate in order to produce fakes. Loch Ness is, naturally enough, fair game for hoaxers of all kinds.

The usual view of an object on the loch is that of a dark image on a light background. This makes the 'negative' fake simplicity itself since all that is needed is to draw a silhouette on the negative or print and then re-photograph the result, so producing an 'original' negative. One of the easiest and most frequently used ways of faking pictures

eyewitness sightings are now on record, thanks to the press, individual authors and investigative organisations such as the Loch Ness Investigation Bureau, which was active between 1962 and 1972. The descriptions are remarkably consistent, and describe a long-necked, hump-backed creature that sometimes moves at speed, both with neck raised and lowered, and at other times simply appears for a while and submerges quietly.

The first chronicler of the Loch Ness sightings was Lieutenant-Commander Rupert Gould who, in his book *The Loch Ness monster* (1934) described 42 sightings from 1923 to 1933 in a well-presented case. He felt that the creature was an isolated specimen that had become trapped in the loch. He was followed by Mrs Constance White, wife of the manager of the Caledonian Canal; her book *More than a legend*, published in 1957, contained references to over 60 sightings. She established that the phenomenon had not ceased after 1934 as some had believed and that sometimes more than one animal was seen at a time – suggesting a resident population. More recent authors include Tim Dinsdale, Ted Holliday, Peter Costello and Nick Witchell, all of whom have added more examples of eyewitness evidence; much of this evidence is drawn from the extensive files of the Loch Ness Investigation Bureau, which collected reports at the loch side.

The sheer volume of eyewitness evidence from Loch Ness and its intensity suggest there is a population of large animals in the water. This and some unexplained scientific findings, particularly through sonar, are all we can go by at present. Surface behaviour is so obviously uncharacteristic that no real pattern can be established. There are more sightings in the summer months, particularly at the mouth of rivers, and certainly more on calm, hot days. But weather conditions and the fact that summer marks the height of the tourist season must be taken into account.

is to photograph ordinary objects out of context. These range from the simple ruse of a pair of motor tyres, with a stone thrown in the water to cause disturbance, to quite sophisticated Loch Ness 'Muppets'. These photographs can, of course, be produced anywhere; background is generally absent since this tends to provide scale and make the object appear smaller and less significant. Where identifiable Loch Ness backgrounds are used, it is common to show existing features that have been slightly adapted, such as rocks in a line, logs or even a fence post adorned with a sock!

From time to time, however, photographs are produced that stimulate real interest. Those dating from 1933 to the present day may be divided into two main types – 'bad' ones that could well be genuine and 'good' ones that are probably not. The 'classic' pictures must be included in any discussion of the Loch Ness phenomenon, although very few are now considered significant evidence by the current Loch Ness and Morar Project. Not only do they differ markedly from one another, but none of the pictures taken during the comprehensive surface study by the Loch Ness Investigation Bureau over a 10-year period shows anything like the amount of body seen in the 'classic' photographs, although some show low-lying humps and wakes.

Ciné films are far harder to fake than still pictures; so, although their subject matter may still be open to debate, they do provide more valuable evidence. Two film sequences in particular are exceptional.

The first was shot on 23 April 1960 by Tim Dinsdale from the mouth of the River Foyers, which flows into Loch Ness from the south about a third of the way up from Fort Augustus. It shows a hump moving slowly away from him and then fast across his field of vision while submerging. The film was submitted to the Joint Air Reconnaissance Intelligence Centre (JARIC) by David James of the Loch Ness Investigation Bureau. In very broad terms, the analysts concluded the object was 'probably animate'. It was nearly $5\frac{1}{2}$ feet (1.7 metres) wide, moved through the water at a speed of about 10mph (16km/h) and appeared to submerge.

The second film, shot by Richard Raynor during the Loch Ness Expedition of 1967 on the morning of 13 June, is exceptional for its technical quality. The film, taken from opposite Dores at the north end of the loch, shows a wake, at the head of which a solid object appears from time to time; the object submerges as a boat enters the field of vision. Raynor is quite ready to entertain the possibility that the animal was an otter (the object was definitely animate); this is really the only possible candidate apart from an unknown animal. However JARIC – especially likely to be accurate in view of the photographic quality – estimates a possible length of 7 feet (2 metres) for the part that breaks the surface; an otter of this proportion would be, to say the least, remarkable.

This film seems to be the best we can expect from surface observation and photography. Although these better examples do suggest that a large animal is involved, they also demonstrate the limitations of this kind of evidence in terms of identification; aquatic creatures cannot be studied on the basis of what proportions of their body are by chance exposed above water.

It was not until 1970 that underwater photography was used as an investigative method. Its potential is enormous, since it should allow a complete profile view of the target to be obtained; in practice, however, the peaty water and limitations of normal underwater equipment reduce the range and coverage drastically. This makes interpretation of underwater pictures very difficult. The most interesting are two computer-enhanced pictures of a finlike object taken in 1972 by Dr Robert Rines of the Academy of Applied Science, Boston, Massachusetts, USA, with a time lapse camera fitted with a strobe flash. Whatever the biological discussions of this evidence, if the object is a fin it does not resemble that of any creature known to inhabit the loch.

Subsequent pictures taken by Rines in

Above: a still from Tim Dinsdale's famous film of 23 April 1960. It is very probably genuine – and, like most genuine photographs of the Loch Ness monster, it shows very little detail

Below: an example of just how misleading perfectly natural objects can sometimes be. The wake shown in this photograph is, experts agree, nothing more than a standing wave left by one of the heavy trawlers that regularly ply the Caledonian Canal, of which Loch Ness forms a part

1975 show six images other than the underside of the boat from which the camera was slung; and it has been suggested that two of these are animate. Other upward shots showing the surface of the loch have brought suggestions of a 'major disturbance' and agitation of the camera. However the time lapse between these 'events' is 70 seconds and one sequence of these surface shots would actually imply that the camera was more or less at rest for at least two minutes rather than swinging. It has been argued that one object, the 'head', has sufficient symmetry to suggest a living creature, with horns used for breathing without creating ripples, although this is obviously a matter of individual interpretation.

Unfortunately, this argument can be countered by the fact that two thirds of the images photographed in the same 24–hour period under the same conditions could by no stretch of the imagination be animate. Either the camera had touched the bottom

Photographs of the Loch Ness expedition of 1972–73: the team at Loch Ness (above); Dr Robert Rines examines one of the underwater cameras used in the search for the monster (left). Led by Dr Rines, the expedition team succeeded in taking the first ever underwater pictures of what was alleged to be the Loch Ness monster. A number of sophisticated techniques were used to obtain the pictures, including the use of sonar to trigger one of the cameras when large objects approached. A second expedition, mounted in 1975, also produced spectacular results, although some still think them controversial

through miscalculation of the depth or it had, in fact, come into contact with inanimate objects in midwater. With the shape of the camera frame and the fact that it would overbalance with the weight of the strobe light clamped above, the camera could tilt up or down if it touched the bottom.

But without doubt the most important class of evidence is that of the echo sounder and sonar. Developed during the Second World War as a submarine detection device, sonar relies on the reflection of transmitted sound waves by underwater targets. It is the only really effective instrument for 'seeing' underwater, particularly where the water is not clear, and by 1960 had been refined to a stage where it was used commercially in fishing – and in the Loch Ness investigations.

By far the most logical and relevant system of enquiry, sonar has also proved the most successful; most reasonably equipped

teams have secured positive contacts with it. The 'hard evidence' that the system has provided is to some extent measurable. The problem, however, is that it requires some expertise to assess the results, and this expertise is not generally found among zoologists. Also, the sonar at present likely to be used in Loch Ness cannot provide graphical representations.

The reflection of sound is caused mainly by the air cavities within a living creature and so an identification on sonar alone is not possible. At best a sonar record is a trace on a paper chart or a blip on a cathode ray tube. Fish shoals, temperature changes and rising gases are all possible causes of sonar contacts. On the positive side, with sonar it is possible to follow the movements of a target under water and to judge from this whether or not it is animate and even to gain some hints as to its identity.

So far teams from Oxford and Cambridge in 1962, Birmingham University in 1968–69, Vickers Oceanics in 1969, the Loch Ness Investigation Bureau between 1969 and 1970, Klein Associates and the Academy of Applied Sciences between 1970 and 1977 and the Partech Company in 1976–77 have all produced results that they consider indicate the presence of an animate contact larger than a salmon and displaying movement and diving rates different from those expected of fish. Some of the results are inconclusive, others positive.

For the most part the teams involved were experienced and in some cases expert; their evidence is not open to dispute, only to investigation. And, as with some of the photographs, attempts to discredit the evidence are as fruitless as overcredulous efforts to identify the type of animals seen.

# A very strange fish?

**What kind of creature is it that can survive in the cold, barren depths of Loch Ness? Where did it come from? Is it a mammal, a reptile or an amphibian? What does it look like?**

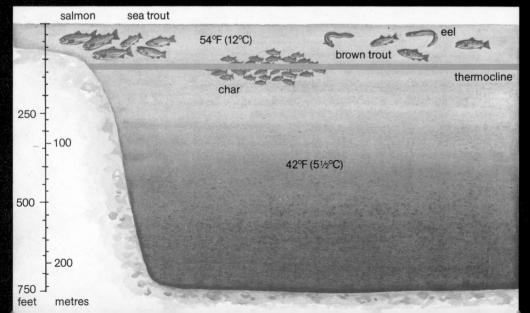

salmon    sea trout

54°F (12°C)

brown trout    eel

char    thermocline

42°F (5½°C)

250
100

500

200

750
feet    metres

Above: Loch Ness with
Castle Urquhart on its
lonely promontory in the
background

Left: a section through
Loch Ness in summer,
showing its fish life,
which is concentrated
close to the surface. Here
the temperature may rise
as high as 54°F (12°C) in
summer. Below a water
layer known as the
thermocline lies the
main body of the loch.
This cold, peaty water
varies in temperature by
no more than half a
degree throughout the
year and supports
virtually no animal life

THERE ARE MANY QUESTIONS that have to be answered in considering Loch Ness as the possible home for one or more large creatures hitherto unidentified. For example, when could they have become established there, how could they exist and – most importantly – what could they possibly be?

Loch Ness, at the northern end of the Great Glen fault line that divides the Highlands of Scotland, is at least 700 feet (over 200 metres) deep and is connected by the River Ness to the sea, which is 52 feet (18 metres) below the level of water in the loch.

Ten thousand years ago, as the ice retreated from the north of Scotland for the last time, the Great Glen fault was opened up to the sea. At some time since then, the surrounding land rose, leaving Loch Ness connected to the sea only by the River Ness.

There is no question of Loch Ness being an evolutionary cul-de-sac, since any creatures that live in the loch must have arrived there after the retreat of the ice 10,000 years ago – a mere blink of the eye in the time-scale of evolution. And these creatures must have come from elsewhere – either from other freshwater areas, or from the sea.

It seems unlikely that any large creature could have entered the loch from freshwater areas – there are not, and never have been, any nearby, and travel to Loch Ness would have entailed considerable distances overland. Thus – and bearing in mind reports of a 'monster' sighted off the coast of Scotland – it seems reasonable to look to the sea for the origins of our creature.

All the larger aquatic species at present living in the loch are capable of migration via the river. The fish are mainly salmonids – salmon, sea trout, brown trout and char – and eels, which spend most of their adult life in fresh water before leaving to breed in the Sargasso Sea. The most likely explanation for the presence of any large unknown species is that it, too, entered from the sea via the River Ness. The salmonid fish, in fact, provide not only a parallel but also an incentive for an unknown species to remain in the loch, as further discussion will show.

## Food for thought

As a habitat the loch is characterised not only by its great size but also by its stability. The majority of water in it does not alter in temperature by more than half a degree from 42°F (5.5°C). In summer the top 100 feet (or 30 metres) may warm up to 54°F (12°C), but this layer remains separated from the unchanged water underneath by what is known as the thermocline.

The potential food sources within the loch are plants, plankton, detritus (organic constituents of sediment) and fish. The dark, peaty water, steep sides and short summer restrict the growth of rooted plants, which are limited for the most part to the first 10 feet (3 metres) of water. Concentrations of bulky plants are close to the shore, so any

Above: a diver gathers material from the loch floor. Analysis of this matter provides an idea of the possible diet of a bottom-dwelling creature

Left: a salmon 'porpoising'. Salmon sometimes put on fantastic bursts of speed as they run up the fast-flowing rivers that lead into Loch Ness to spawn. Could it be that they are being chased by the Loch Ness monster?

creature feeding off these would be seen more often than recorded sightings suggest. All herbivorous animals require a very considerable volume of food to survive and the scarcity of aquatic vegetation in the loch rules out these species.

Some of the world's largest animals are plankton feeders – for instance, the largest mammal, the blue whale, and the largest fish, the basking and whale sharks – and it could be that the 'monster' also feeds on plankton. In general, however, the Scottish lochs are oligotrophic, which means they are very deep in relation to their surface area and are characterised by relative sterility. They also have sparse amounts of plankton compared to other lakes without 'monster' traditions, such as those in the Lake District. Plankton feeders exhibit physical adaptations for capturing and straining plankton from the water. Whales, for example, have baleen brushes and some fish have gills adapted as strainers. These feeders also possess large mouths to take in the greatest possible volume of water, which by all accounts does not seem to apply to our long-necked animal. They also display a great deal of surface activity, since it is near the surface that plankton is concentrated; this is also contrary to the evidence we have so far of our unknown species.

Detritus, as already mentioned, is the organic matter present in the deposits on the loch floor. Some coarse fish are detrital feeders, while others feed on the invertebrates and insect larvae found in or on the sides of the loch. In general the deposits on the floor of Loch Ness are not rich in organic material; samples taken from the loch floor show that organic material makes up 15 to 30 per cent of the total. Special observations were made at Loch Morar by divers briefed to look for signs of large animals feeding on the sediment to depths of up to 100 feet (or 30 metres). The divers were sent down in those areas found to have the greatest concentrations of organic matter, but they found no such traces. In themselves, however, these findings are not sufficient to rule out the possibility that unknown animals might find a suitable food source here, since a community

of invertebrates was discovered living within the sediment at depths of 1,000 feet (300 metres) in Loch Morar. But the majority of evidence is against this theory.

By far the most likely food source for a large animal is the migratory salmonid fish. Although there is a good resident population of brown trout and eels that grow to maturity in Loch Ness, it remains true that the loch is a rather sterile place from a biological point of view. The productivity of any enclosed body of water involves a food chain beginning with the chemical nutrients entering the water and the amount of light available for photosynthesis. These, together with the degree of water circulation, set the limit for the phytoplankton (microscopic plants), which then limit the zooplankton (microscopic animals) that feed upon it. The zooplankton in turn, together with the insect

Left: the leatherback turtle, seen here returning to the sea off Malaya after laying its eggs. It has been argued that the Loch Ness monster could not possibly be a reptile, as a cold-blooded creature – one whose body temperature depends on its environment – could not survive in the loch. The leatherback turtle, however, can live in the chilliest seas, and has even been found off the coast of Scotland

Below: a ringed seal off the snowy coast of Greenland. Seals can survive in the coldest waters; this fact has been used to support the theory that the Loch Ness monster could be a mammal

larvae and invertebrates in the mud on the bottom, become food for the fish population. Little in the way of nutrients enters the loch since the seven main rivers that flow into it – Oich, Tarff, Foyers, Farigaig, Enrick, Coiltie and Morriston – run rapidly over rocky terrain, picking up little from the smooth, stony river bed.

### Chasing the salmon

It seems to rest with the salmon and sea trout to provide a solution to the food supply problem. The salmon hatch in rivers entering the loch and remain in fresh water for the first two years of their life, attaining a weight of up to 9 ounces (250 grams). They then leave for the sea for up to three years before returning to the same place to spawn. At this point in the cycle, they weigh anything up to 40 pounds (18 kilograms), all of the energy for this growth being derived from outside the loch's food chain. While in fresh water the salmon do not eat and do not therefore act as a drain on the loch's existing food resources; only in those first years must the young salmon (or parr) rely on the food chain. Mature salmon are present virtually all the year round, since they enter at different times – although mainly in spring and summer.

Some aspects of reported behaviour support the theory of a fish-predator. Sightings are frequently made off the mouths of rivers in spate, when the salmon are running up to spawn and recorded bursts of high speed would be consistent with an animal chasing the fish. If there is a large unknown animal species in the loch, it is reasonable to expect it to exploit this special bonus to the food chain – the salmonid fish.

One objection to the existence of a Loch Ness 'monster' has always been the absence of floating or beached remains. Animals are often recognised by science on the basis of their remains long before a living specimen is observed. Père David obtained the skin of a giant panda in 1869, but it was 50 years

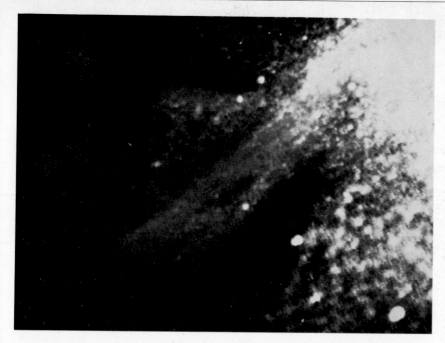

before the first one was seen alive by westerners (and promptly shot) in 1929. There are few records of strange carcases being found at Scottish lochs – and none of them recent. Loch Ness and Loch Morar are deep, steep-sided and cold, and it is particularly the depth that is relevant since the water pressure would slow down decomposition and allow time for eels to dispose of the remains. This probably accounts for Loch Ness's reputation for 'never giving up its dead'.

Many reptiles and mammals, both terrestrial and aquatic, have the curious habit of swallowing small stones. It seems that they use this additional weight as ballast, particularly when swimming near the surface where pressure due to water is insufficient to keep the animal submerged. Seals, for instance, have been found with up to 25 pounds (11 kilograms) of stones in their guts. This may also have some significance in the argument that the 'monster' is a reptile or a mammal – if it, too, swallows stones as ballast, these will cause its body to sink to the bottom of the loch after its death.

Exactly what the 'monster' is – if it exists at all – is the most interesting question of all. The presence of an adapted marine fish-predator within the loch is not, in itself, particularly remarkable. What is remarkable is that it seems to be an unknown animal. Furthermore, some of its 'characteristics' raise difficulties no matter what class of animal is considered. It is precisely these features, which make it hard for the zoologist to believe in the 'monster', that will make it such an interesting find.

The largest known invertebrate is the giant squid, until recently itself a 'mythical' animal. Very few of the sightings in Loch Ness could apply to the squid, quite apart from the fact that there are no known freshwater representatives of the family. Were it not for the fact that until recently Loch Ness

Above: Dr Robert Rines's famous 'monster flipper' photograph, taken in 1972. If this is indeed part of the Loch Ness monster, it provides some interesting information about what kind of creature it is. The photograph shows a rhomboid flipper with a clear central 'rib' – which, experts agree, is not an efficient design for swimming

Right: comparison with the fin of a fish (top left) and a sea-lion flipper (top right) reveals that the structure of the 'monster flipper' is entirely different. In fact, the nearest parallel is the fin of the Australian lungfish (bottom): this, too, has a clear central stiffening – but it is used mainly for crawling along the sea bed

was an arm of the sea, an amphibian would seem a reasonable candidate. Amphibians do not need to breathe often and they hibernate and reproduce in water. The problem is that there are not, and palaeontology indicates that there never have been, any marine amphibians. Therefore if we are right in expecting to find the origins of our 'monster' at sea, we are probably not looking for an amphibian.

## Reptile, mammal or fish?

Certainly the most popular theory is that the 'monster' is a reptile. However, the biological objections are strong. The temperature of the loch would seem too cold for a reptile to remain active. Also a reptile would have to surface in order to breathe and would be expected to come ashore to lay eggs. Of course there are always exceptions to prove the rule. Freshwater 'turtles', for example, can sometimes be seen swimming beneath the ice covering North American lakes (although Loch Ness itself does not freeze). The leatherback turtle, by virtue of its size, maintains its temperature above that of its surroundings and has been caught at sea off the west coast of Scotland. And sea snakes bear their young alive in the water.

The reptile most often suggested as fitting the 'descriptions' is the plesiosaur. On the precedent of the coelacanth, absent from

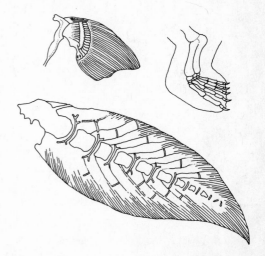

fossil records for 70 million years yet found alive and well in the Indian Ocean in 1938, the mere fact that the plesiosaur has been 'extinct' for a similar period does not deter its advocates. And it is conceivable that this type of animal could have adapted to cope with the difficulties of the loch already mentioned. Secondarily aquatic reptiles and mammals have waterproof skins and breathing apparatus – that is, lungs as opposed to gills. Their systems are therefore isolated from the water, which gives them some immunity from osmotic stress caused by moving from salt to fresh water, or vice versa; this makes long-term adaptation to fresh water easier. Creatures with permeable skins and using gills for breathing would normally suffer from the change, since the fresh water would cause an imbalance as it entered through the skin and gills into the existing body fluids.

From an environmental point of view, a mammal is a more probable bet. Most seals, for example, are perfectly at home in low temperatures, and a long-necked seal could account for some of the sightings. The problem of reproduction remains, however, since seals breed – and in general give birth – on land. And the need to breathe frequently – and therefore to surface – should not allow a population of this kind to remain so elusive.

The least unlikely solution would be a

Below: the Australian lungfish, whose fins provide the closest parallel to the 'monster flipper' of Dr Robert Rines's photograph that can be found among known living creatures

fish, which would certainly account for the rare surface appearances and take care of the reproduction as well. Unfortunately, most sighting reports do not seem to describe a fish, although there could be something in the opinion among locals that the 'monster' is a large eel of known or unknown species. Some of the sonar evidence suggests that contacts rise and return to the bottom, which is consistent with the behaviour of the eel or of the European catfish, both of which become active at night. The apparent tendency to surface in calm, hot weather, which was first noted by Pontoppidan of the 'sea serpent' in 1752 and is supported by testimonies at Loch Ness, is consistent with the behaviour of bottom-dwelling fish. At least they make rather 'extrovert' surface appearances in response to barometric pressure changes. This is true not only of the catfish but also of the European pond loach – or weather fish – which has, in fact, been used as a living barometer.

The 'flipper' picture taken in 1972 by Dr Robert Rines is interesting, if it is indeed part of an unknown animal. The flipper or fin is of a rhomboid shape, which led Rines and Sir Peter Scott, the naturalist, to suggest the scientific name *Nessiteras rhombopteryx* for the animal. It has been pointed out that the shape of this flipper makes it inefficient for aquatic propulsion. Efficient limbs, like those of the plesiosaur, sea lion and even the penguin, all have the rigid bones up at the leading edge, thus enabling the rest of the

Below: a model of the plesiosaur, the reptile that seems most nearly to fit the descriptions of the Loch Ness monster. The plesiosaur is thought to have been extinct for the past 70 million years – but that in itself does not automatically rule out the possibility that this *is* the monster. A rare fish, the coelacanth, was also thought to have been extinct for millions of years – until one was found in the Indian ocean in 1938

flipper to flex; this provides propulsion in precisely the same way as a diver's flipper. The 'flipper' picture shows a central 'rib', suggesting that propulsion would come from the flipper folding on the forward stroke and stiffening on the backward stroke, the mechanism for which is not apparent. Alternatively, the flipper would have to be rotated, or slewed, on the forward stroke, although again there is no obvious stiffening sufficient for this. This leads one to conclude that the flipper is not a prime source of propulsion, since power would be lost on one stroke rather than being gained on both as with a true flipper; this in turn would eliminate the plesiosaur as a candidate. The animal would therefore have to be propelled by its tail, with the flipper possibly functioning for steering – or even as a brake.

If the flipper is considered as part of a fish, in which case it would be appropriate to call it a fin, the position is different. Accepting the objection that the fin is inefficient for aquatic propulsion, fish are anyway almost always tail-propelled and many species have put their fins to other uses apart from swimming. The nearest parallel to the 'monster' flipper of Rines's photograph known in nature is, in fact, the fin of an Australian lungfish, which has a clear central stiffening and functions as a leg for crawling along the bottom. It could therefore be argued that the flipper is more likely to be the fin of a bottom-roving fish than the propulsive flipper of a reptile or mammal.

Whatever the Loch Ness 'monster' may turn out to be – and we do not at present have enough information to suggest any animal group with confidence – there will be some very interesting questions to be answered, far more interesting than the mere discovery of a 'monster'. If it is an amphibian, how did it invade the loch in the first place? If a reptile, how does it cope with the cold? If a mammal, how does it remain so elusive? And if it is a fish, it is indeed a very strange fish.

# Creatures of the Irish lakes

**The countless lakes and bogs of Ireland have yielded many sightings of large creatures of unknown species. JANET and COLIN BORD describe ancient legends and modern reports that tell of these monsters**

THE BEST-KNOWN LAKE MONSTER in the world must surely be the one in Loch Ness, and many people suppose that 'Nessie' is unique. But if there really is a monster (or, more likely, a family of monsters) in Loch Ness, then why not in other lakes? According to reports by many reliable eyewitnesses, there are. Scottish lochs other than Loch Ness are reputed to hide monsters, for example 'Morag' of Loch Morar; and not far away across the Irish Sea many of Ireland's lakes, large and small, have over the years been the location of strange sightings. The reports have not come solely from 20th-century witnesses who might be jealous of Nessie's fame and hope to encourage tourists to visit Ireland's lakes. Stories of evil water monsters are part of Irish legend. Sometimes called *piast, peiste, payshtha, ollphiast* or *ullfish*, these water demons were said to be horse-like – hence another name still used today, horse-eel.

The 12th-century *Leabhar na h'Uidhre* ('Book of the dun cow') tells the story of a huge *piast* that lived in an unfathomable lakelet, Slieve Mis, in County Kerry. This beast was in the habit of emerging to make meals of the people and cattle living in a *cashel*, or stone-walled fort, on the shores of the lake. The Irish hero Cuchulain was close by one night when he heard it coming and, contrary to what one might expect of a hero, and indicating the terror that the *piast* aroused in him, he leapt over the wall into the cashel, out of reach of the monster. It was left to certain Irish saints to tangle with the water demons. St Mochua of Balla got the better of a monster in one of the loughs of Connaught, while St Senanus and St Kevin were successful in their struggles with the *piasts* of Scattery and Glendalough. St Patrick tricked

Right: lough monsters are today most commonly seen in County Kerry and the Connemara district of Galway

Bottom: Lough Ree, near Athlone, in which three priests watched a monster one day, in May 1960

the monster of a southern Irish lough into imprisoning itself beneath a large vat, while St Colman of Dromore rescued a girl who was swallowed by a monster while washing her nightdress in a pool. From the number of old legends and stories that mention lake monsters, it is clear that belief in them was widespread.

A description from the 10th-century *Book of Lismore* compares interestingly with recent sighting reports. The anonymous author has exaggerated his monster, but certain features are echoed in the 20th-century reports – a repulsive appearance, noticeable eyes, forked tail, existence on land or in the water, the inability of boats (and, of course, humans other than saints) to catch it, and a horse-like appearance. From both Ireland and Scotland come traditions of water horses, which look so much like real horses that people seeing them often mistook them for land horses. Legend tells that, in County Cavan, enchanted water horses would come out of Lough Ramor at night and graze on the oats in a farmer's field. He managed to catch a foal and trained it to work on his farm, but one evening as he rode it beside the lake, the water horses neighed and the foal plunged into the water, carrying the farmer with it. Neither was seen again. The same fate befell a boy working near Lough Caogh in County Leitrim, who captured what he thought was a stray horse and used it to harrow a field. After a while it ran back into the lake, taking harrow and boy with it.

Although such stories as these are far-fetched and should not be considered as descriptions of actual events, they may indicate that people in past centuries saw monsters in the loughs just as people do

Above: Cuchulain, hero of Irish mythology. He is said to have encountered a huge lough monster in County Kerry, so terrifying that it frightened even him away

Above right: Patrick, the fifth-century missionary to Ireland who became the island's patron saint. Born in Britain, he was captured by Irish raiders at the age of 16 and was a slave until his escape six years later. He returned to Ireland and converted the country to Christianity. According to legend he not only captured a lough monster, but blessed the shamrock, banished snakes, and defeated the druids in feats of magical skill

Left: the *Book of Lismore*, dating from the 10th century. The manuscript has a detailed description of a lough monster, 'repulsive, outlandish, fierce and very terrifying'. It had the front end of a horse, iron claws, a fiery breath, and the tail fins of a whale, with iron nails on them. The sea would boil when this fearsome monster rushed into the water. Boats could not catch it and 'no-one escaped to tell the tale of it, from then till now . . .'

today and that, observing horse-like features, they wove tall tales around the facts. Some of the factual reports that follow liken the appearance of the monster's *head* to a horse's, but sometimes from a distance even today's monsters look entirely horse-like. Patrick Canning saw what he described as 'a lovely black foal' beside Lough Shanakeever in County Galway around 1955. He had gone to fetch his donkey out of the rain, and from about 200 yards (180 metres) he saw a black animal, the size of a foal, circling round the donkey. It had a long neck, and he also saw a head with ears. As he approached, it went into the water. Lough Shanakeever is the scene of many other sightings; these will be described later. Meanwhile, here are reports of some of the monsters that have been seen in the loughs around Ireland.

### The monster of Lough Muck

Towards the end of the 19th century, a strange animal was occasionally seen in Lough Muck in County Donegal. Around 1885, a young woman had waded into the lough to pull bog-bean. Hearing a splash, she looked round and saw a big-eyed monster heading for her through the water. Not unnaturally, she got ashore as quickly as possible.

Lough Muck's monster was seen again in the following few years, its two humps above the water. One very strange fact is that Lough Muck is less than three-quarters of a mile (1 kilometre) long and half a mile (800 metres) across, and it is not the only small lake in Ireland where monsters have been seen. In such small areas of water, there is a very limited food supply, consisting mainly of fish such as brown trout. Later we shall return to this enigma – which initially seems to suggest that it would be impossible for large monsters to live in these loughs.

Lough Abisdealy in County Galway is another small lake, only 1 mile (1.6 kilometres) long by a quarter-mile (400 metres) wide. An Irish name for the lake translates as 'the lake of the monster', and there was a tradition that a water horse lived in it. A monster was reportedly seen during the Crimean War of 1854–56; then, in 1914, just before the outbreak of the First World War, it appeared again. Three people driving to church in a dogcart saw it as they passed close to the lake. It was long and black, long-necked and with a flat head held high, and two loops of its body moved in and out of the water as it travelled quickly across the lake, looking like a gigantic snake. On another occasion, at night, a man saw a huge eel-like creature crawling out of the lake.

It is always possible that a monster may attack witnesses – and this thought evidently went through the mind of Georgina Carberry, who with friends saw a monster in Lough Fadda, County Galway in 1954. Miss Carberry was the librarian at Clifden, and in the 1960s she told monster hunter F. W. Holiday about her frightening experience. She and her three friends were on a fishing expedition to the small lough – 1½ miles (2.4 kilometres) long and only 600 yards (550 metres) at its widest point – and by the time they pulled their boat on shore for a tea-break, they had caught several trout. Then one of the four noticed what looked at first like a man swimming in the water. But as it slowly got closer, they could see that it looked like nothing they knew. When it was only 20 yards (18 metres) away, they apprehensively moved back from the water's edge. Miss Carberry remembered the creature's open mouth quite clearly – 'a huge great mouth', which was white inside. The monster's body was 'wormy . . . creepy', and 'seemed to have movement all over it all the

Above: Lough Muck in County Donegal, one of the smaller Irish lakes, in which a two-humped monster was seen several times towards the end of the 19th century

Below: part of the Connemara district of County Galway. It is dotted with lakes hewn from the ice rock by ancient ice sheets, and is covered with peat bog. Most of the lakes are too small to support a large creature

time'. The head stood high above the water on a long neck, and as the watchers moved back the creature dived round a rock, showing a forked tail. When it surfaced further up the lake, they could see two humps out of the water behind its head. The shock of the sighting caused Miss Carberry to have nightmares for weeks afterwards. Such a reaction is not surprising, of course. Most of us could not easily cope with a sudden encounter with an unknown monster. Its horrible appearance, and its apparent intention, as it heads open-mouthed towards the witness, of grabbing a quick meal of tasty human flesh, are enough to give anyone nightmares. But the monster that swims towards lake-shore watchers may only be curious, like cows that wander across a field to stare at people. The

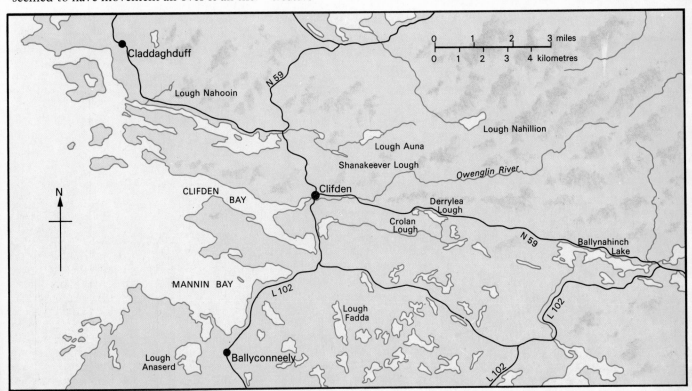

monsters are also likely to be harmless herbivores.

On 18 May 1960, three Dublin priests fishing in the waters of Lough Ree watched a long-necked, flat-headed animal swimming in the water only 100 yards (90 metres) away. It was a warm, calm evening, and the men saw the creature quite clearly. The head and neck, between 18 and 24 inches (45 and 60 centimetres) long, were separated by about 2 feet (60 centimetres) of water from another part of the body that could have been a hump on the back of a large creature beneath the water surface. They watched for two or three minutes as the creature swam slowly towards the shore. It then gradually submerged, reappearing a couple of minutes later and then disappearing again 30 yards (27 metres) from the shore.

## A monster attacks

So far, we have described long-necked creatures with undulating bodies, but the creature seen in Lough Dubh near Glinsk, County Galway, by school-teacher Alphonsus Mullaney and his son does not fit this description at all. The lake was known to be a monster haunt. Three men had seen a strange animal there around 1956, while in 1960 three monsters were seen, one large and two smaller. It was in March 1962 that Mr Mullaney and his son had their encounter, and Mr Mullaney described to a newspaper reporter what happened:

We were working on the bog after school and I had promised to take young Alphonsus fishing. We carried a twelve foot [4-metre] rod with a strong line and spoon bait for perch or pike, of which there are plenty in Lough Dubh.

For a while I let the boy fish with the rod and used a shorter rod with worm bait. I got no 'answer'. After five minutes I decided that the fish were not there that evening, but I took the long rod and walked up and down the bank.

Suddenly there was a tugging on the line. I thought it might be on a root, so I took it gently. It did not give. I hauled

Above: Georgina Carberry, an expert angler who encountered a lough monster

Below: the monster of Lough Fadda, as described by Miss Carberry and her companions

Bottom: Lough Fadda, County Galway, set in a wilderness of bogs

it slowly ashore, and the line snapped. I was examining the line when the lad screamed.

Then I saw the animal. It was not a seal or anything I had ever seen. It had for instance short thick legs, and a hippo face. It was as big as a cow or an ass, square faced, with small ears and a white pointed horn on its snout. It was dark grey in colour, and covered with bristles or short hair, like a pig.

Young Alphonsus screamed because the monster, apparently having taken the bait and in pain, had tried to get out of the lough and attack him. Father and son escaped, and Mr Mullaney alerted local men who took guns to the lake – but nothing was seen.

During the 1960s, the number of sighting reports increased, perhaps because of a generally growing interest in lake monsters. Some investigators visited the Irish loughs to carry out experiments, and they also talked to local people who had seen strange animals. Because so many of the loughs are small and remote, they are rarely visited, unlike Loch Ness, which has 40 miles (65 kilometres) of motor road around it, frequently patrolled by goggle-eyed tourists. It is usually local people or fishermen who see the Irish lough monsters – no one else visits the loughs.

W. J. Wood was fishing on Lough Attariff

in County Cork in June 1966 when a long, dark brown object suddenly surfaced about 100 yards (90 metres) away. It was facing him, and Mr Wood reported that 'it had the head of a well-grown calf and large glittering eyes almost at water-level.' After a couple of minutes it submerged. In 1967 the same witness saw a light, yellowish brown 'monster', about 7 feet (2 metres) long, which surfaced only a few yards from him when he was fishing in Lackagh Lake in County Kerry. When F. W. Holiday visited the area he found that a young man living nearby had seen a snake-like neck several feet long, topped by a small head with two stumpy horns, and the sight had scared the life out of him.

A more recent sighting has also come from a remote County Kerry lake, Lough Brin, which is 5 miles (8 kilometres) from a metalled road and approachable only along a rough

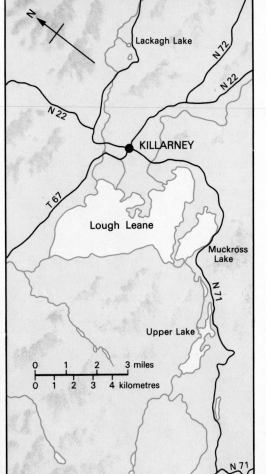

Above: Lough Dubh, scene of several monster sightings, which culminated in an attack on Alphonsus Mullaney

Right: the Lough Dubh creature, described as being covered with bristles and having a hippo-like face with a horn on its snout

Left: the area around Killarney, in County Kerry, scene of monster sightings

Right: the reptilian creature seen in Lough Brin, reconstructed from the accounts of two witnesses

Below: an invocation from this youthful witch at Lough Keane, County Kerry, in 1980 succeeded in attracting a photographer but failed to raise a water monster

track. Not surprisingly, its only visitors are local farmers. A monster has been seen there in past years, and in the summer of 1979 two farmers saw a reptilian creature something like a cross between a giant seal and the mythical dragon. It was as black as soot and about 10 feet (3 metres) long, and they watched it swim along the length of the 500-yard (450-metre) lough before submerging.

If lake monsters could be summoned up from their murky depths, the raging controversy as to whether they are real could be easily resolved.

**The country folk of western Ireland tell of strange lake creatures – the 'water horses', 'water eels' or peistes – that are frequently seen there**

THE IRISH LOUGHS where lake monsters have been seen are very small – too small, it might seem, to support large mysterious creatures. But would-be monster catchers face fewer problems in searching one of these than in confronting Loch Ness, a huge body of water, 22 miles (35 kilometres) long.

In the 1960s a researcher into the lake monsters of Connemara in County Galway, Captain Lionel Leslie, tried some experiments in monster raising. His first was in October 1965 at Lough Fadda, where Georgina Carberry had a clear sighting of a 'creepy' monster while fishing in 1954. Captain Leslie got permission to detonate gelignite at Lough Fadda. His intention was to create a large shock-wave that would disturb the monster and cause it to surface. He set 5 pounds (2 kilograms) of explosive against the rock where Miss Carberry had seen the monster at close range. Ten seconds after it exploded, the Captain and his companions saw a large, blackish object surface amid much splashing about 50 yards (45 metres) away. Unfortunately not much detail could be seen because of the splashing, but they saw enough to convince them that there

Above: the monster of Lough Nahooin, in an artist's impression based on descriptions given by the seven members of the Coyne family

Below: Lough Nahooin, a tiny peat tarn in County Galway. Stephen Coyne (inset) was the first to see the mysterious creature on that memorable evening in February 1968

was a monster in the lake, still very much alive.

Captain Leslie's next plan was to net Lough Fadda, and he was able to do this in October 1967. The net was in place for a couple of weeks, but nothing was caught. Storms prevented Leslie from dragging the lake for the monster.

Nothing daunted, in 1968 Captain Leslie laid plans to search other Irish loughs where monsters had been seen. This time he worked with a large team of monster hunters. The lough finally chosen for netting was Lough Nahooin, near Claddaghduff in County Galway. It was a tiny lake, only about 100 yards (90 metres) long and 80 yards (73 metres) wide, and the chances of catching the monster seemed very high. They were certain that there was a monster

# The perplexing Irish peiste

in the lake because a local farmer, Stephen Coyne, had seen it on 22 February 1968, only five months before the netting operation. Mr Coyne was out gathering peat at the lakeside in the early evening, accompanied by his eight-year-old son and their dog. Seeing a black object in the water, Mr Coyne whistled to it, thinking it was his dog. To his surprise the dog came running along from behind him, stopped on seeing the creature in the water, and began to bark. The creature swam towards the shore, mouth open, apparently responding to the dog's barking (and perhaps thinking of supper?), but when Mr Coyne went over to join the dog, the monster changed direction and swam around the lake.

Mr Coyne sent his son to fetch the rest of the family, and soon he was joined by his wife and four other children. They watched the monster for a while, and before the light failed they were able to see it clearly enough to describe it in some detail. Its closest approach to them was between 5 and 10 yards (4.5 and 9 metres). It was about 12 feet (3.5 metres) long, black and hairless, with an eel-like texture to the skin. They caught glimpses of a tail, and when the monster put its head underwater two humps appeared. The neck was pole-like and about 12 inches (30 centimetres) in diameter. The interior of the mouth was pale, and the creature had two 'horns' on top of its head. Neither Mr nor Mrs Coyne noticed any eyes. The monster seen by Georgina Carberry in Lough Fadda had a pale mouth; one seen in Lackagh Lake had two stumpy horns; and humps are often reported. Stephen Coyne told the monster hunters that he had also seen a monster in the lake 20 years earlier. It had rolled over and he had seen its pale underbelly.

The netting operation began at Lough

Left: Tommy Joyce at his house overlooking Shanakeever Lough, where he saw a mysterious creature

Below: the disturbance of these reeds, seen here from Tommy Joyce's position during the sighting, gave him an impression of the bulk of the creature

Nahooin on 15 July 1968, and by 17 July a line of nets stretched across the entire width of the lake. Only 23 feet (7 metres) deep at its deepest part, where Mr Coyne had seen the monster appear on both occasions, the lake proved much easier to net than would Loch Ness, 800 to 900 feet (240 to 275 metres) deep. The only similarity between the lakes, apart from their reputation as monster haunts, is the peat in the water, which makes it dark and visually impenetrable.

David James had an electronic fish-attracting device with him, but neither that nor the 'monster rousers' (empty petrol tins containing pebbles, pulled through the water on a rope) succeeded in raising a monster. The nets remained empty and Professor Mackal did not need his harpoon gun, which he was hoping to use to obtain a tissue sample from the monster. The team members could

spare only a few days in Ireland and so the experiment unfortunately ended in failure.

However, in 1969 Captain Leslie, Ivor Newby, F. W. Holiday and others decided to try again. This time they netted three loughs – Nahooin once again, Shanakeever, and Auna. Auna and Shanakeever were inter-connected, and both of them had been reported to contain monsters.

About the turn of the century, a woman saw a 'horse-eel' come out of Lough Auna and on to the turf bank very close to where she was working. She did not wait to see what happened next!

Some years later, a man stacking peat by the lough saw a humped creature with a length of 30 to 40 feet (9 to 12 metres) rolling in the water. It seemed to have a mane or fin along its neck.

Patrick Canning's 1950s sighting of a

## The thing in Lough Auna

A sighting of a lough monster crowned a summer barbecue party held in 1980 by Air Commodore Kort, a retired officer of the Royal Netherlands Air Force, now resident in County Galway. The party took place at Mr Kort's cottage in County Limerick. He and his guests had just retired indoors when he saw an odd shape moving through the waters of nearby Lough Auna. With a guest,

Right: the form seen by Air Commodore Kort and Mr Adrian O'Connell gliding through the waters of Lough Auna one May evening

Below: the westward motion of the creature carried it into the reeds. It had been seen by at least three watchers

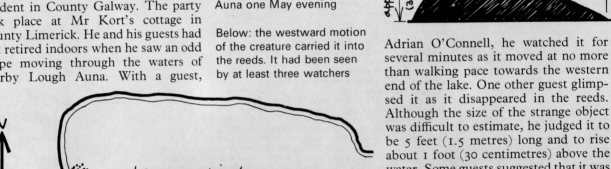

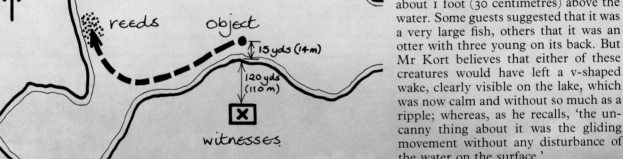

Adrian O'Connell, he watched it for several minutes as it moved at no more than walking pace towards the western end of the lake. One other guest glimpsed it as it disappeared in the reeds. Although the size of the strange object was difficult to estimate, he judged it to be 5 feet (1.5 metres) long and to rise about 1 foot (30 centimetres) above the water. Some guests suggested that it was a very large fish, others that it was an otter with three young on its back. But Mr Kort believes that either of these creatures would have left a v-shaped wake, clearly visible on the lake, which was now calm and without so much as a ripple; whereas, as he recalls, 'the uncanny thing about it was the gliding movement without any disturbance of the water on the surface.'

black creature on the shore of Shanakeever Lough was described as 'a lovely black foal'. In either 1963 or 1964 Tommy Joyce, an alert local farmer, saw a dark grey object about $7\frac{1}{2}$ feet (2.5 metres) long in the water among the reeds of the same lough.

These sightings were all reported to the monster-hunting team, who were able to meet and talk to most of the witnesses. The investigators had no doubts about the witnesses' veracity and became convinced that they had seen something strange. So, despite the failure of earlier netting attempts, they began their 1969 experiments with confidence. Even at Lough Nahooin, where they had found no trace of a monster in 1968, they were keen to try again, since they had heard of a sighting there that took place only a month before. On 8 September a sheep farmer, Thomas Connelly, saw a black creature, bigger than a young donkey, on the lake shore a few yards from the water's edge. It seemed to have four stumpy legs, and was slithering towards the lake. As Connelly watched, the monster moved into the water and sank. This sighting has strong echoes of Patrick Canning's beside Shanakeever Lough, where he saw a creature resembling a black foal.

Unfortunately, an attempt to drag Lough Nahooin with chains failed because they kept getting caught in the thick water lilies. The nets stretched across all three loughs remained in place and the monsters shyly remained hidden. The persistent but unlucky hunters, assailed by wind and rain,

Above: the loughs and bogs of Connemara. Seen from the air, the countryside is a patchwork of small lakes set in broad areas of peat. The lake creatures may be amphibious, moving from lough to lough at night and feeding on the land as well as in the water

Right: two generations ago, children were kept away from Lough Crolan, in Connemara, because of the 'horse-eels' that had been seen in it. In 1961 Tom Connelly, a local man, watched an eel-like creature with a 'velvety' skin, at least 12 feet (4 metres) long, rising and sinking repeatedly in one spot for over half an hour.

realised that they were not going to catch their monster.

From all the evidence, it seems clear that the so-called 'lake monsters' are amphibious and can live as well on land as in water. The Loch Ness monster has been seen on land several times, and so have the monsters in a number of the Irish sightings. The monsters are obviously happier in water, as it conceals them so well. But when disturbed, as by hunters, they appear to slip out of the lough and make their way across the bog to another stretch of water. This would not be too

difficult a feat in Connemara where there are vast areas of uninhabited bogs and many small lakes.

That the monsters do leave the loughs is also suggested by two reports from Connemara, dating from the end of the 19th century. The first described an 'oversized eel' that got jammed in the culvert connecting Crolan Lough with Derrylea Lough, and died there, its corpse being left to rot away. At Ballynahinch, a spear was made to kill a 30-foot (9-metre) monster trapped under a bridge. But before the men could kill it, a flood occurred one night and carried the lucky creature away with it.

Such tales as these are frustrating to monster hunters, whose attempts to catch, or even glimpse, a monster invariably meet with failure. Even more frustrating are recent reports of close sightings of monsters on land. Why is it that monsters are almost always seen by people who are not expecting them, who react by running away, and who never have a ciné camera to hand? For example, in 1968 the monster of Sraheens Lough on Achill Island, County Mayo, was very active. The lake was known as a monster haunt, sightings having been made there in the 1930s and in 1966. Yet again the lake is small, only about 1200 feet (365 metres) in circumference, and therefore unlikely to be

Below: the monster of Sraheens Lough was seen three times in 10 days in May 1968. Twice it appeared on land, and was terrifying enough to scare the witnesses away

able to supply a monster with food for very long. Two local men, Michael McNulty and John Cooney, came upon the monster at night on 1 May 1968, while driving home. As they passed the lough, a strange creature ran across the road only a few yards ahead of the car and then disappeared into the thick undergrowth. They could see it clearly in the car's headlights, and what they saw made the driver step on the accelerator, with no thought of stopping to investigate! Eight to ten feet (2½ to 3 metres) long and about 2½ feet (75 centimetres) tall, the animal had a long thick tail, a long neck, and a head like a sheep or greyhound. It was a shiny dark brown in

colour, and as it ran it rocked from side to side.

Only a week later, 15-year-old Gay Dever saw the monster in daylight. He was cycling by Sraheens Lough when he heard a splashing noise on the shore. Stopping to look, he was amazed to see a large black animal crawling out of the water. It was much bigger than a horse, and had a long neck, a sheep-like head, a tail and four legs, the hind ones being the biggest. Gay Dever's reaction was to leave the scene without delay.

Two days later, the monster was allegedly seen yet again, by two girls trying to hitch-hike home to Achill Sound. They were waiting near the lough and as a car stopped for them, one of the girls turned back towards the lough. By the light of the full Moon she and the driver saw a monster.

F. W. Holiday, who researched deeply into lake monsters, wrote that there are 'at least 50 credible accounts' of monsters seen on land. But there is a lack of food for so many monsters in small Irish loughs, and the failure of determined hunters to prove conclusively the existence of even one lake monster after years of concentrated effort made him wonder whether these monsters are not just large aquatic animals, but might also have a paranormal aspect. On numerous occasions monsters appeared immediately after observers had put their cameras away, or else the cameras jammed. The comment he made in 1976 is still relevant: 'Monsters are certainly a fact; but they are not the sort of fact we first supposed.'

Above: John Cooney who, with a companion, saw the Sraheens monster in the headlights of his car

Left: nearly a century ago, a large ell-like creature was trapped in a culvert leading from Lough Crolan into Lough Derrylea. The carcase was so loathsome that no one would remove it and it was left to decompose

# Delusions and transformations

**History abounds with stories of people who claim to be werewolves, and behave in a savage and bestial way – and yet keep their human shape. This form of madness still occurs today. IAN WOODWARD seeks an explanation**

MOST PEOPLE'S CONCEPTION of a werewolf is of an excessively hairy and ferocious man-beast that walks upright on two legs, growls and foams at the mouth, and displays large, dirty-looking lupine teeth. This, of course, is the now familiar portrait represented by late-night television movies like *Curse of the werewolf*, *The wolf man* and *Legend of the werewolf* – and it is inaccurate in all essentials.

History and mythology are quite clear in describing a man transformed into a werewolf as being little different from a natural wolf, except perhaps slightly larger than the wild species.

Those unfamiliar with the subject also tend to bracket werewolves with lycanthropes and talk about them as if they were one and the same thing. They are not.

A *lycanthrope* is a mentally sick person who believes that he has assumed the shape, voice and behaviour of a wolf, although he has not actually undergone any physical transformation. In the 15th and 16th centuries it was believed that the werewolf's fur grew on the inside of his skin; and many a lycanthrope has given this explanation when asked why, if he is a wolf, he still looks exactly like a person.

A *werewolf*, on the other hand, is traditionally a man who, by the agency of magic or by natural inclination, possesses an ability to change his shape to that of a wolf. All the characteristics associated with that animal – the ferocity, strength, cunning and swiftness – are readily displayed, to the dumbfounded

Above: Oliver Reed stars in the Hammer film *The curse of the werewolf*, made in 1960. Typically, this movie werewolf is quite unlike its traditional original; it remains clothed and walks upright

Below: 'the gleaming eyes of the classic werewolf dream', in a 1930s illustration by Peter Coccogna for the American magazine *Fantasy Fiction*. Some writers have suggested that werewolves are astral projections from lycanthropic dreams

horror of all whose path he crosses. He may remain in his animal form for a few hours or even permanently.

When Peter Stump, a notorious German 'werewolf' who died a terrible death near Cologne in 1589, confessed to magical self-transformation, we may be inclined to think him as fanatical as his judges were credulous. But having killed, mutilated and devoured hundreds of human and animal victims – though he admitted to only 16 people – while convinced he was to all intents and purposes a wolf, we can be in no doubt at all that he was suffering from the madness called lycanthropy.

'Lycanthropy' and 'lycanthrope' derive directly from the Greek words *lycos*, meaning 'wolf', and *anthropos*, meaning 'man'. Although lycanthropy originally referred to the ancient phenomenon of men capable of undergoing animal metamorphosis, a phenomenon fervently believed in by such ancient Greek physicians as Cribasios and Aetios, it gradually became a term applied exclusively to men who *imagined* they had effected transformation into wild beasts of prey. For this reason, lycanthropy is looked upon by psychiatrists as a fundamental delusion.

As for the werewolf proper, two qualities were said to remain when a man was transformed into a wolf: his human voice and his eyes. But in all other respects the metamorphosed werewolf was entirely animal: he had the hairy skin and claws of a wild wolf.

In his human form, however, a number of physical characteristics distinguished the werewolf from his fellow men. His eyebrows were said to meet on the bridge of the nose, and his long, almond-shaped fingernails were of a 'sickening' blood-red tinge; the third finger, in particular, was always very long. The ears, which were positioned rather

Right: the life of Peter Stump, Germany's infamous werewolf, in a 16th-century woodcut. While in wolf form, he would seek out young women working in the fields and, changing back into his human shape, would rape them, then murder and devour them. It was alleged that he tore unborn babies from their mothers' wombs, gulping down the hearts 'panting hot and raw'. He was eventually brought to justice in 1589, and confessed to having made a pact with the Devil, who had taught him the art of shape-changing and provided him with a wolf's skin for the purpose. The final pictures show his torture, and execution with his wife and daughter

low down and to the back of the head, and a tendency towards hairiness of the hands and feet, were also clear identifying marks.

There are traditionally three principal types of werewolf. The first was the *hereditary werewolf*. His involuntary malady was passed down from one generation to another as a consequence of some terrible family curse. The second was the *voluntary werewolf*. His depravity of mind led him by choice to the realms of black-magic ritual, and to the use of all manner of terrible charms, potions, ointments, girdles, animal skins and Devil-worship incantations to bring about the desired metamorphosis. And the third was the *benevolent werewolf*. This gentle, protective scion of the werewolf family is almost a contradiction in terms. He felt nothing but shame for his brutal appearance and wished that no harm should befall man or animal. Two of the most familiar benevolent werewolves are depicted in a fine pair of 12th-century romances, *William and the werewolf*

Below: the benevolent werewolf of the late-12th-century Breton *Lay of the bisclaveret*, by Marie de France, in an illustration from Frank Hamel's *Human animals* of 1915. The poem tells the story of one of Brittany's finest knights, who spends three days of every week as a werewolf – but has no savage instincts, except against his unfaithful wife and her lover. In the end, the wife outwits her husband by persuading her lover to steal his clothes – without which the werewolf cannot regain human form

by Guillaume de Palerne and Marie de France's *Lay of the bisclavaret* (*bisclavaret* is the Breton term for the Norman *varulf*, or werewolf), about one of Brittany's most gallant knights.

The medieval theory was that, while the werewolf kept his human form, his hair grew inwards; when he wished to become a wolf, he simply turned himself inside out. An examination of the many verbatim trial documents reveals that the prisoners – undoubtedly lycanthropes – were painstakingly questioned in a bid to discover the 'secrets' of animal metamorphosis. When such interrogation failed and the patience of the judges ran out, some wretched victim would invariably have his arms and legs cut off, or be partly flayed, in an attempt to find the reputed inward-growing hair.

## Haunters of shadowy woods

Another theory was that the possessed person had merely to put on a wolf's skin in order to assume instantly the lupine form and character. There is a vague similarity here with the alleged fact that the berserker – the Scandinavian bear-man or *werebear* – haunted the shadowy woods at night clothed in the hides of wolves or bears to acquire superhuman strength by transformation.

Such a skin was kept by a half-witted wolf-boy called Jean Grenier. Jacques Rollet, a sixteenth-century lycanthrope, confessed to using a magic salve or ointment, as he admitted in court on 8 August 1598.

'What are you accused of having done?' asked the judge.

'Of having offended God,' replied the 35-year-old accused werewolf. 'My parents gave me an ointment; I do not know its composition.'

Then the judge asked, 'When rubbed with

# A change for the worse

Why is it that so many werewolf stories stem from medieval times? One theory suggests that the fact cannot be explained away by pointing to the superstitious nature of the medieval mind: biochemically-induced hallucinations may have been almost everyday experiences for many people.

Extracts from the skins of toads, and plants such as mandrake, henbane and deadly nightshade, or belladonna, were frequently used by practitioners of the secret arts to induce sensations of flying or the delusion of growing claws and nails and turning into an animal.

But such hallucinations were not available only to people who *chose* to take these drugs. In medieval mills, grain was sorted into two heaps: clean grain for the aristocracy and clergy, and *ergotised* grain for the peasants. Ergotised grain carries a fungus that produces lysergic acid diethylamide – a drug similar to LSD that also produces the illusion of being turned into an animal. Thus almost anyone, at any time, could suddenly feel himself turning into – a werewolf.

Below: Charles Leadbeater, an early Theosophist, who made a study of astral projection in his book *The astral plane* (1895), and believed that the idea of the astral body was of central importance in understanding the werewolf phenomenon

this ointment, do you become a wolf?'

'No,' Rollet replied, 'but for all that, I killed and ate the child Cornier: I was a wolf.'

'Were you dressed as a wolf?'

'I was dressed as I am now. I had my hands and my face bloody, because I had been eating the flesh of the said child.'

'Do your hands and feet become the paws of a wolf?'

'Yes, they do.'

'Does your head become like that of a wolf – your head become larger?'

'I do not know how my head was at the time; I used my teeth; my head was as it is today. I have wounded and eaten many other little children.'

A further method of becoming a werewolf was to obtain a girdle, usually of animal origin, but occasionally made from the skin of a hanged man. Such a girdle was fastened with a buckle having seven tongues. When the buckle was unclasped, or the girdle cut, the charm was dissolved.

One account tells of a 16th-century sorcerer who possessed such a girdle. One day he went away from the house for a few hours without remembering to lock up the girdle. His young son subsequently climbed up to the cupboard to get it, and, as he was buckling it around his waist, he was instantly transformed into a 'strange-looking beast'. At this point, his father returned home and, on seizing the girdle, restored the child to his former natural shape.

It is said that the boy confessed that no

Below: the famous 19th-century French occultist Eliphas Levi, who suggested that, in certain cases, while people lay in bed having nightmares about being wolves, their 'sidereal bodies' would wander the countryside in the form of werewolves

sooner had he buckled the girdle than he was tormented with a fierce hunger and a bestial rage. But it seems more likely that, being of a susceptible age, he had heard his father boast of the girdle's magical qualities and was determined to 'experience' them for himself.

Eliphas Levi, the leading French occultist of the 19th century, who once collapsed in terror as a result of his own remarkable 'transcendental' magic, has explained the process of werewolfic transformation as a 'sympathetic condition between man and his animal presentment [form]'. He rightly notes in *History of magic* (1860) that werewolves, though tracked down, hunted and even maimed, have never been killed on the spot; and that people suspected of these atrocious self-transformations have always been found at home, after the pursuit of the werewolf, more or less wounded, sometimes dying, but in their natural form.

### Savage and sanguinary instincts

Levi then goes on to discuss the phenomenon of man's 'sidereal body' – 'the mediator between the soul and the material organism' – and uses it as the basis of an explanation of werewolfism:

This body remains awake very often while the other is asleep, and by thought transports itself through all space which universal magnetism opens to it. It thus lengthens, without breaking, the sympathetic chain attaching it to the heart and brain. The form of our sidereal body is conformable to the habitual condition of our thoughts, and in the long run it is bound to modify the features of the material organism.

Levi proceeds to suggest that the werewolf is nothing more than the sidereal body of a man whose savage and sanguinary instincts are represented by the wolf, who, while his phantom is wandering abroad, dreams that he is nothing less than a savage wolf.

Certainly Theosophists today believe that during the Middle Ages, when public execution was common, many people sank so low morally that their astral bodies, the human spirits that we are said to use after death, actually linked with an animal. This explains why, if the astral body were to manifest itself in the form of a wolf, and it were subsequently wounded – its paw cut off, say, by a hunter – that wound would be duplicated on the werewolf's physical body in its human form: that is, one of the hands would be badly wounded or missing when the werewolf reverted to its human state.

Charles Webster Leadbeater, an Anglican

Above: Rose Gladden, a British clairvoyant and healer who has dealt with many cases of werewolfism. She believes that the werewolf is an astral projection that has been transformed by evil into the shape of a wolf

certainly a theory that is gaining considerable ground among many of today's spiritual thinkers. Rose Gladden, one of Britain's most experienced exorcists and a renowned clairvoyant healer, has no doubt that the diabolical application of astral projection played a key role in the lives of many accused werewolves. She explains:

Suppose I was a cruel person who enjoyed the horrible things in life – well, as I projected my astral body out of my physical body, all the surrounding evil could grasp me. And it would be the evil grasping my astral projection, or grasping my 'double', which would transform me into an animal, into a wolf.

The atmosphere is always full of evil forces, and these evil forces find it much easier to exist within mankind – within an evil man, say – than in a nebulous vacuum. People addicted to werewolfery were – indeed, still are – the most evil manifestations of humanity. I can well understand why there are so many instances on record of 'wound-doubling'.

### A strange restlessness

Among the countless number of wound-doubling reports on historical record is one concerning a German farmer and his wife who were hay-making near Caasburg in the summer of 1721. After a while the wife said that she felt an unconquerable restlessness: she could not remain there a minute longer; she would have to go away.

After making her husband promise that if any wild animal came near he would throw his hat at it and run away, she quickly disappeared. But she had not been gone many seconds when a wolf was seen to be swimming across the nearby stream and heading for the hay-makers. The farmer threw his hat at the beast, which tore it to bits; but before he could make a hasty retreat, a man stole round with a pitchfork and stabbed the wolf to death. The beast's form changed instantly . . . and everyone was horrified to see that the man had slain the farmer's wife.

Whether fact or fancy, killing a werewolf in this way has always, by tradition, been the most favoured means by which to force him (or her) to resume his natural form on the spot, or lead to his speedy detection. But the bizarre episodes of wound-doubling often reported in werewolf cases are also common in out-of-the-body experiences. Could it be that this remarkable fact points towards a possible explanation of the werewolf superstition – astral projection? Is a werewolf no more than a manifestation of the 'sidereal body' spoken of by Eliphas Levi – a man's projected phantom?

Above: a werewolf attacks a man while his friend looks on, horrified and powerless to help, in a 16th-century woodcut from *Die Emeis* by Johann Geiler von Kaiserberg

clergyman who lived at the turn of the century and became one of the principal figures of the Theosophical Society, substantiates with great enthusiasm the theory of wound-doubling in his book *The astral plane* (1895):

As so often with ordinary materialisation, any wound inflicted upon that animal will be reproduced upon the human physical body by the extraordinary phenomenon of repercussion; though after the death of that physical body, the astral (which will probably continue to appear in the same form) will be less vulnerable. It will then, however, be also less dangerous, as unless it can find a suitable medium it will be unable to materialise fully.

The phenomenon of wound-doubling, through the agency of astral projection, is